The Red Record

by

Ida B. Wells-Barnett

The Echo Library 2005

Published by

The Echo Library

Paperbackshop Ltd
Cockrup Farm House
Coln St Aldwyns
Cirencester GL7 5AZ

www.echo-library.com

ISBN 1-84637-592-4

The Red Record: Tabulated Statistics and Alleged Causes of Lynching in the United States
By Ida B. Wells-Barnett

1895

PREFACE

HON. FREDERICK DOUGLASS'S LETTER

DEAR MISS WELLS:

Let me give you thanks for your faithful paper on the lynch abomination now generally practiced against colored people in the South. There has been no word equal to it in convincing power. I have spoken, but my word is feeble in comparison. You give us what you know and testify from actual knowledge. You have dealt with the facts with cool, painstaking fidelity, and left those naked and uncontradicted facts to speak for themselves.

Brave woman! you have done your people and mine a service which can neither be weighed nor measured. If the American conscience were only half alive, if the American church and clergy were only half Christianized, if American moral sensibility were not hardened by persistent infliction of outrage and crime against colored people, a scream of horror, shame, and indignation would rise to Heaven wherever your pamphlet shall be read.

But alas! even crime has power to reproduce itself and create conditions favorable to its own existence. It sometimes seems we are deserted by earth and Heaven—yet we must still think, speak and work, and trust in the power of a merciful God for final deliverance.

Very truly and gratefully yours,
FREDERICK DOUGLASS
Cedar Hill, Anacostia, D.C.

4

CONTENTS

1

THE CASE STATED

The student of American sociology will find the year 1894 marked by a pronounced awakening of the public conscience to a system of anarchy and outlawry which had grown during a series of ten years to be so common, that scenes of unusual brutality failed to have any visible effect upon the humane sentiments of the people of our land.

Beginning with the emancipation of the Negro, the inevitable result of unbribled power exercised for two and a half centuries, by the white man over the Negro, began to show itself in acts of conscienceless outlawry. During the slave regime, the Southern white man owned the Negro body and soul. It was to his interest to dwarf the soul and preserve the body. Vested with unlimited power over his slave, to subject him to any and all kinds of physical punishment, the white man was still restrained from such punishment as tended to injure the slave by abating his physical powers and thereby reducing his financial worth. While slaves were scourged mercilessly, and in countless cases inhumanly treated in other respects, still the white owner rarely permitted his anger to go so far as to take a life, which would entail upon him a loss of several hundred dollars. The slave was rarely killed, he was too valuable; it was easier and quite as effective, for discipline or revenge, to sell him "Down South."

But Emancipation came and the vested interests of the white man in the Negro's body were lost. The white man had no right to scourge the emancipated Negro, still less has he a right to kill him. But the Southern white people had been educated so long in that school of practice, in which might makes right, that they disdained to draw strict lines of action in dealing with the Negro. In slave times the Negro was kept subservient and submissive by the frequency and severity of the scourging, but, with freedom, a new system of intimidation came into vogue; the Negro was not only whipped and scourged; he was killed.

Not all nor nearly all of the murders done by white men, during the past thirty years in the South, have come to light, but the statistics as gathered and preserved by white men, and which have not been questioned, show that during these years more than ten thousand Negroes have been killed in cold blood, without the formality of judicial trial and legal execution. And yet, as evidence of the absolute impunity with which the white man dares to kill a Negro, the same record shows that during all these years, and for all these murders only three white men have been tried, convicted, and executed. As no white man has been lynched for the murder of colored people, these three executions are the only instances of the death penalty being visited upon white men for murdering Negroes.

Naturally enough the commission of these crimes began to tell upon the public conscience, and the Southern white man, as a tribute to the nineteenth-century civilization, was in a manner compelled to give excuses for his barbarism. His excuses have adapted themselves to the emergency, and are aptly outlined by that greatest of all Negroes, Frederick Douglass, in an article of recent date, in which he shows that there have been three distinct eras of Southern barbarism, to account for which three distinct excuses have been made.

The first excuse given to the civilized world for the murder of unoffending Negroes was the necessity of the white man to repress and stamp out alleged "race riots." For years immediately succeeding the war there was an appalling slaughter of colored people, and the wires usually conveyed to northern people and the world the intelligence, first, that an insurrection was being planned by Negroes, which, a few hours later, would prove to have been vigorously resisted by white men, and controlled with a resulting loss of several killed and wounded. It was always a remarkable feature in these insurrections and riots that only Negroes were killed during the rioting, and that all the white men escaped unharmed.

From 1865 to 1872, hundreds of colored men and women were mercilessly murdered and the almost invariable reason assigned was that they met their death by being alleged participants in an insurrection or riot. But this story at last wore itself out. No insurrection ever materialized; no Negro rioter was ever apprehended and proven guilty, and no dynamite ever recorded the black man's protest against oppression and wrong. It was too much to ask thoughtful people to believe this transparent story, and the southern white people at last made up their minds that some other excuse must be had.

Then came the second excuse, which had its birth during the turbulent times of reconstruction. By an amendment to the Constitution the Negro was given the right of franchise, and, theoretically at least, his ballot became his invaluable emblem of citizenship. In a government "of the people, for the people, and by the people," the Negro's vote became an important factor in all matters of state and national politics. But this did not last long. The southern white man would not consider that the Negro had any right which a white man was bound to respect, and the idea of a republican form of government in the southern states grew into general contempt. It was maintained that "This is a white man's government," and regardless of numbers the white man should rule. "No Negro domination" became the new legend on the sanguinary banner of the sunny South, and under it rode the Ku Klux Klan, the Regulators, and the lawless mobs, which for any cause chose to murder one man or a dozen as suited their purpose best. It was a long, gory campaign; the blood chills and the heart almost loses faith in Christianity when one thinks of Yazoo, Hamburg, Edgefield, Copiah, and the countless massacres of defenseless Negroes, whose only crime was the attempt to exercise their right to vote.

But it was a bootless strife for colored people. The government which had made the Negro a citizen found itself unable to protect him. It gave him the right to vote, but denied him the protection which should have maintained that right. Scourged from his home; hunted through the swamps; hung by midnight raiders, and openly murdered in the light of day, the Negro clung to his right of franchise with a heroism which would have wrung admiration from the hearts of savages. He believed that in that small white ballot there was a subtle something which stood for manhood as well as citizenship, and thousands of brave black men went to their graves, exemplifying the one by dying for the other.

The white man's victory soon became complete by fraud, violence, intimidation and murder. The franchise vouchsafed to the Negro grew to be a "barren ideality," and regardless of numbers, the colored people found themselves voiceless in the councils of those whose duty it was to rule. With no longer the fear of "Negro Domination" before their eyes, the white man's second excuse became valueless. With the Southern governments all subverted and the Negro actually eliminated from all participation in state and national elections, there could be no longer an excuse for killing Negroes to prevent "Negro Domination."

Brutality still continued; Negroes were whipped, scourged, exiled, shot and hung whenever and wherever it pleased the white man so to treat them, and as the civilized world with increasing persistency held the white people of the South to account for its outlawry, the murderers invented the third excuse—that Negroes had to be killed to avenge their assaults upon women. There could be framed no possible excuse more harmful to the Negro and more unanswerable if true in its sufficiency for the white man.

Humanity abhors the assailant of womanhood, and this charge upon the Negro at once placed him beyond the pale of human sympathy. With such unanimity, earnestness and apparent candor was this charge made and reiterated that the world has accepted the story that the Negro is a monster which the Southern white man has painted him. And today, the Christian world feels, that while lynching is a crime, and lawlessness and anarchy the certain precursors of a nation's fall, it can not by word or deed, extend sympathy or help to a race of outlaws, who might mistake their plea for justice and deem it an excuse for their continued wrongs.

The Negro has suffered much and is willing to suffer more. He recognizes that the wrongs of two centuries can not be righted in a day, and he tries to bear his burden with patience for today and be hopeful for tomorrow. But there comes a time when the veriest worm will turn, and the Negro feels today that after all the work he has done, all the sacrifices he has made, and all the suffering he has endured, if he did not, now, defend his name and manhood from this vile accusation, he would be unworthy even of the contempt of mankind. It is to this charge he now feels he must make answer.

If the Southern people in defense of their lawlessness, would tell the truth and admit that colored men and women are lynched for almost any offense, from murder to a misdemeanor, there would not now be the necessity for this defense. But when they intentionally, maliciously and constantly belie the record and bolster up these falsehoods by the words of legislators, preachers, governors and bishops, then the Negro must give to the world his side of the awful story.

A word as to the charge itself. In considering the third reason assigned by the Southern white people for the butchery of blacks, the question must be asked, what the white man means when he charges the black man with rape. Does he mean the crime which the statutes of the civilized states describe as such? Not by any means. With the Southern white man, any mesalliance existing between a white woman and a colored man is a sufficient foundation for the charge of rape. The Southern white man says that it is impossible for a voluntary alliance to exist between a white woman and a colored man, and therefore, the fact of an alliance is a proof of force. In numerous instances where colored men have have been lynched on the charge of rape, it was positively known at the time of lynching, and indisputably proven after the victim's death, that the relationship sustained between the man and woman was voluntary and clandestine, and that in no court of law could even the charge of assault have been successfully maintained.

It was for the assertion of this fact, in the defense of her own race, that the writer hereof became an exile; her property destroyed and her return to her home forbidden under penalty of death, for writing the following editorial which was printed in her paper, the *Free Speech*, in Memphis, Tenn., May 21,1892:

Eight Negroes lynched since last issue of the *Free Speech* one at
Little Rock, Ark., last Saturday morning where the citizens broke(?)
into the penitentiary and got their man; three near Anniston, Ala., one
near New Orleans; and three at Clarksville, Ga., the last three for
killing a white man, and five on the same old racket—the new alarm
about raping white women. The same programme of hanging, then shooting
bullets into the lifeless bodies was carried out to the letter. Nobody
in this section of the country believes the old threadbare lie that
Negro men rape white women. If Southern white men are not careful, they
will overreach themselves and public sentiment will have a reaction; a
conclusion will then be reached which will be very damaging to the moral
reputation of their women.

But threats cannot suppress the truth, and while the Negro suffers the soul deformity, resultant from two and a half centuries of slavery, he is no more guilty of this vilest of all vile charges than the white man who would blacken his name.

During all the years of slavery, no such charge was ever made, not even during the dark days of the rebellion, when the white man, following the fortunes of war went to do battle for the maintenance of slavery. While the master was away fighting to forge the fetters upon the slave, he left his wife and children with no protectors save the Negroes themselves. And yet during those years of trust and peril, no Negro proved recreant to his trust and no white man returned to a home that had been dispoiled.

Likewise during the period of alleged "insurrection," and alarming "race riots," it never occurred to the white man, that his wife and children were in danger of assault. Nor in the Reconstruction era, when the hue and cry was against "Negro Domination," was there ever a thought that the domination would ever contaminate a fireside or strike to death the virtue of womanhood. It must appear strange indeed, to every thoughtful and candid man, that more than a quarter of a century elapsed before the Negro began to show signs of such infamous degeneration.

In his remarkable apology for lynching, Bishop Haygood, of Georgia, says: "No race, not the most savage, tolerates the rape of woman, but it may be said without reflection upon any other people that the Southern people are now and always have been most sensitive concerning the honor of their women—their mothers, wives, sisters and daughters." It is not the purpose of this defense to say one word against the white women of the South. Such need not be said, but it is their misfortune that the chivalrous white men of that section, in order to escape the deserved execration of the civilized world, should shield themselves by their cowardly and infamously false excuse, and call into question that very honor about which their distinguished priestly apologist claims they are most sensitive. To justify their own barbarism they assume a chivalry which they do not possess. True chivalry respects all womanhood, and no one who reads the record, as it is written in the faces of the million mulattoes in the South, will for a minute conceive that the southern white man had a very chivalrous regard for the honor due the women of his own race or respect for the womanhood which circumstances placed in his power. That chivalry which is "most sensitive concerning the honor of women" can hope for but little respect from the civilized world, when it confines itself entirely to the women who happen to be white. Virtue knows no color line, and the chivalry which depends upon complexion of skin and texture of hair can command no honest respect.

When emancipation came to the Negroes, there arose in the northern part of the United States an almost divine sentiment among the noblest, purest and best white women of the North, who felt called to a mission to educate and Christianize the millions of southern exslaves. From every nook and corner of the North, brave young white women answered that call and left their cultured homes, their happy associations and their lives of ease, and with heroic determination went to the South to carry light and truth to the benighted blacks. It was a heroism no less than that which calls for volunteers for India, Africa and the Isles of the sea. To educate their unfortunate charges; to teach them the Christian virtues and to inspire in them the moral sentiments manifest in their own lives, these young women braved dangers whose record reads more like fiction than fact. They became social outlaws in the South. The peculiar sensitiveness of the southern white men for women, never shed its protecting influence about them. No friendly word from their own race cheered them in their work; no hospitable doors gave them the companionship like that from which they had come. No chivalrous white man doffed his hat in honor or respect. They were "Nigger teachers"—unpardonable offenders in the social ethics of the South, and were insulted, persecuted and ostracised, not by Negroes, but by the white manhood which boasts of its chivalry toward women.

And yet these northern women worked on, year after year, unselfishly, with a heroism which amounted almost to martyrdom. Threading their way through dense forests, working in schoolhouse, in the cabin and in the church, thrown at all times and in all places among the unfortunate and lowly Negroes, whom they had come to find and to serve, these northern women, thousands and thousands of them, have spent more than a quarter of a century in giving to the colored people their splendid lessons for home and heart and soul. Without protection, save that which innocence gives to every good woman, they went about their work, fearing no assault and suffering none. Their chivalrous protectors were hundreds of miles away in their northern homes, and yet they never feared any "great dark-faced mobs," they dared night or day to "go beyond their own roof trees." They never complained of assaults, and no mob was ever called into existence to avenge crimes against them. Before the world adjudges the Negro a moral monster, a vicious assailant of womanhood and a menace to the sacred precincts of home, the colored people ask the consideration of the silent record of gratitude, respect, protection and devotion of the millions of the race in the South, to the thousands of northern white women who have served as teachers and missionaries since the war.

The Negro may not have known what chivalry was, but he knew enough to preserve inviolate the womanhood of the South which was entrusted to his hands during the war. The finer sensibilities of his soul may have been crushed out by years of slavery, but his heart was full of gratitude to the white women of the North, who blessed his home and inspired his soul in all these years of freedom. Faithful to his trust in both of these instances, he should now have the impartial ear of the civilized world, when he dares to speak for himself as against the infamy wherewith he stands charged.

It is his regret, that, in his own defense, he must disclose to the world that degree of dehumanizing brutality which fixes upon America the blot of a national crime. Whatever faults and failings other nations may have in their dealings with their own subjects or with other people, no other civilized nation stands condemned before the world with a series of crimes so peculiarly national. It becomes a painful duty of the Negro to reproduce a record which shows that a large portion of the American people avow anarchy, condone murder and defy the contempt of civilization. These pages are written in no spirit of vindictiveness, for all who give the subject consideration must concede that far too serious is the condition of that civilized government in which the spirit of unrestrained outlawry constantly increases in violence, and casts its blight over a continually growing area of territory. We plead not for the colored people alone, but for all victims of the terrible injustice which puts men and women to death without form of law. During the year 1894, there were 132 persons executed in the United States by due form of law, while in the same year, 197 persons were put to death by mobs who gave the victims no opportunity to make a lawful defense. No comment need be made upon a condition of public sentiment responsible for such alarming results.

The purpose of the pages which follow shall be to give the record which has been made, not by colored men, but that which is the result of compilations made by white men, of reports sent over the civilized world by white men in the South. Out of their own mouths shall the murderers be condemned. For a number of years the *Chicago Tribune*, admittedly one of the leading journals of America, has made a specialty of the compilation of statistics touching upon lynching. The data compiled by that journal and published to the world January 1, 1894, up to the present time has not been disputed. In order to be safe from the charge of exaggeration, the incidents hereinafter reported have been confined to those vouched for by the Tribune.

2

LYNCH-LAW STATISTICS

From the record published in the *Chicago Tribune*, January 1, 1894, the following computation of lynching statistics is made referring only to the colored victims of Lynch Law during the year 1893:

ARSON

Sept. 15, Paul Hill, Carrollton, Ala.; Sept. 15, Paul Archer, Carrollton, Ala.; Sept. 15, William Archer, Carrollton, Ala.; Sept. 15, Emma Fair, Carrollton, Ala.

SUSPECTED ROBBERY

Dec. 23, unknown negro, Fannin, Miss.

ASSAULT

Dec. 25, Calvin Thomas, near Brainbridge, Ga.

ATTEMPTED ASSAULT

Dec. 28, Tillman Green, Columbia, La.

INCENDIARISM

Jan. 26, Patrick Wells, Quincy, Fla.; Feb. 9, Frank Harrell, Dickery, Miss.; Feb. 9, William Filder, Dickery, Miss.

ATTEMPTED RAPE

Feb. 21, Richard Mays, Springville, Mo.; Aug. 14, Dug Hazleton, Carrollton, Ga.; Sept. 1, Judge McNeil, Cadiz, Ky.; Sept. 11, Frank Smith, Newton, Miss.; Sept. 16, William Jackson, Nevada, Mo.; Sept. 19, Riley Gulley, Pine Apple, Ala.; Oct. 9, John Davis, Shorterville, Ala.; Nov. 8, Robert Kennedy, Spartansburg, S.C.

BURGLARY

Feb. 16, Richard Forman, Granada, Miss.

WIFE BEATING

Oct. 14, David Jackson, Covington, La.

ATTEMPTED MURDER

Sept. 21, Thomas Smith, Roanoke, Va.

ATTEMPTED ROBBERY

Dec. 12, four unknown negroes, near Selma, Ala.

RACE PREJUDICE

Jan. 30, Thomas Carr, Kosciusko, Miss.; Feb. 7, William Butler, Hickory Creek, Texas; Aug. 27, Charles Tart, Lyons Station, Miss.; Dec. 7, Robert Greenwood, Cross county, Ark.; July 14, Allen Butler, Lawrenceville, Ill.

THIEVES

Oct. 24, two unknown negroes, Knox Point, La.

ALLEGED BARN BURNING

Nov. 4, Edward Wagner, Lynchburg, Va.; Nov. 4, William Wagner, Lynchburg, Va.; Nov. 4, Samuel Motlow, Lynchburg, Va.; Nov. 4, Eliza Motlow, Lynchburg, Va.

ALLEGED MURDER

Jan. 21, Robert Landry, St. James Parish, La.; Jan. 21, Chicken George, St. James Parish, La.; Jan. 21, Richard Davis, St. James Parish, La.; Dec. 8, Benjamin Menter, Berlin, Ala.; Dec. 8, Robert Wilkins, Berlin, Ala.; Dec. 8, Joseph Gevhens, Berlin, Ala.

ALLEGED COMPLICITY IN MURDER

Sept. 16, Valsin Julian, Jefferson Parish, La.; Sept. 16, Basil Julian, Jefferson Parish, La.; Sept. 16, Paul Julian, Jefferson Parish, La.; Sept. 16, John Willis, Jefferson Parish, La.

MURDER

June 29, Samuel Thorp, Savannah, Ga.; June 29, George S. Riechen, Waynesboro, Ga.; June 30, Joseph Bird, Wilberton, I.T.; July 1, James Lamar, Darien, Ga.; July 28, Henry Miller, Dallas, Texas; July 28, Ada Hiers, Walterboro, S.C.; July 28, Alexander Brown, Bastrop, Texas; July 30, W.G. Jamison, Quincy, Ill.; Sept. 1, John Ferguson, Lawrens, S.C.; Sept. 1, Oscar Johnston, Berkeley, S.C.;

Sept. 1, Henry Ewing, Berkeley, S.C.; Sept. 8, William Smith, Camden, Ark.; Sept. 15, Staples Green, Livingston, Ala.; Sept. 29, Hiram Jacobs, Mount Vernon, Ga.; Sept. 29, Lucien Mannet, Mount Vernon, Ga.; Sept. 29, Hire Bevington, Mount Vernon, Ga.; Sept. 29, Weldon Gordon, Mount Vernon, Ga.; Sept. 29, Parse Strickland, Mount Vernon, Ga.; Oct. 20, William Dalton, Cartersville, Ga.; Oct. 27, M.B. Taylor, Wise Court House, Va.; Oct. 27, Isaac Williams, Madison, Ga.; Nov. 10, Miller Davis, Center Point, Ark.; Nov. 14, John Johnston, Auburn, N.Y.

Sept. 27, Calvin Stewart, Langley, S.C.; Sept. 29, Henry Coleman, Denton, La.; Oct. 18, William Richards, Summerfield, Ga.; Oct. 18, James Dickson, Summerfield, Ga.; Oct. 27, Edward Jenkins, Clayton county, Ga.; Nov. 9, Henry Boggs, Fort White, Fla.; Nov. 14, three unknown negroes, Lake City Junction, Fla.; Nov. 14, D.T. Nelson, Varney, Ark.; Nov. 29, Newton Jones, Baxley, Ga.; Dec. 2, Lucius Holt, Concord, Ga.; Dec. 10, two unknown negroes, Richmond, Ala.; July 12, Henry Fleming, Columbus, Miss.; July 17, unknown negro, Briar Field, Ala.; July 18, Meredith Lewis, Roseland, La. July 29, Edward Bill, Dresden, Tenn.; Aug. 1, Henry Reynolds, Montgomery, Tenn.; Aug. 9, unknown negro, McCreery, Ark.; Aug. 12, unknown negro, Brantford, Fla.; Aug. 18, Charles Walton, Morganfield, Ky; Aug. 21, Charles Tait, near Memphis, Tenn.; Aug. 28, Leonard Taylor, New Castle, Ky; Sept. 8, Benjamin Jackson, Quincy, Miss.; Sept. 14, John Williams, Jackson, Tenn.

SELF-DEFENSE

July 30, unknown negro, Wingo, Ky.

POISONING WELLS

Aug. 18, two unknown negroes, Franklin Parish, La.

ALLEGED WELL POISONING

Sept. 15, Benjamin Jackson, Jackson, Miss.; Sept. 15, Mahala Jackson, Jackson, Miss.; Sept. 15, Louisa Carter, Jackson, Miss.; Sept. 15, W.A. Haley, Jackson, Miss.; Sept. 16, Rufus Bigley, Jackson, Miss.

INSULTING WHITES

Feb. 18, John Hughes, Moberly, Mo.; June 2, Isaac Lincoln, Fort Madison, S.C.

MURDEROUS ASSAULT

April 20, Daniel Adams, Selina, Kan.

NO OFFENSE

July 21, Charles Martin, Shelby Co., Tenn.; July 30, William Steen, Paris, Miss.; Aug. 31, unknown negro, Yarborough, Tex.; Sept. 30, unknown negro, Houston, Tex.; Dec. 28, Mack Segars, Brantley, Ala.

ALLEGED RAPE

July 7, Charles T. Miller, Bardwell, Ky.; Aug. 10, Daniel Lewis, Waycross, Ga.; Aug. 10, James Taylor, Waycross, Ga.; Aug. 10, John Chambers, Waycross, Ga.

ALLEGED STOCK POISONING

Dec. 16, Henry G. Givens, Nebro, Ky.

SUSPECTED MURDER

Dec. 23, Sloan Allen, West Mississippi.

SUSPICION OF RAPE

Feb. 14, Andy Blount, Chattanooga, Tenn.

TURNING STATE'S EVIDENCE

Dec. 19, William Ferguson, Adele, Ga.

RAPE

Jan. 19, James Williams, Pickens Co., Ala.; Feb. 11, unknown negro, Forest Hill, Tenn.; Feb. 26, Joseph Hayne, or Paine, Jellico, Tenn.; Nov. 1, Abner Anthony, Hot Springs, Va.; Nov. 1, Thomas Hill, Spring Place, Ga.; April 24, John Peterson, Denmark, S.C.; May 6, Samuel Gaillard, ——, S.C.; May 10, Haywood Banks, or Marksdale, Columbia, S.C.; May 12, Israel Halliway, Napoleonville, La.; May 12, unknown negro, Wytheville, Va.; May 31, John Wallace, Jefferson Springs, Ark.; June 3, Samuel Bush, Decatur, Ill.; June 8, L.C. Dumas, Gleason, Tenn.; June 13, William Shorter, Winchester, Va.; June 14, George Williams, near Waco, Tex.; June 24, Daniel Edwards, Selina or Selma, Ala.; June 27, Ernest Murphy, Daleville, Ala.; July 6, unknown negro, Poplar Head, La.; July 6, unknown negro, Poplar Head, La.; July 12, Robert Larkin, Oscola, Tex.; July 17, Warren Dean, Stone Creek, Ga.; July 21, unknown negro, Brantford, Fla.; July 17, John Cotton, Connersville, Ark.; July 22, Lee Walker, New Albany, Miss.; July 26, —— Handy, Suansea, S.C.; July 30, William Thompson, Columbia, S.C.; July 28, Isaac Harper, Calera, Ala.; July 30, Thomas Preston, Columbia, S.C.; July 30, Handy Kaigler, Columbia, S.C.; Aug. 13, Monroe Smith, Springfield, Ala.; Aug. 19, negro tramp, near Paducah, Ky.; Aug.

21, John Nilson, near Leavenworth, Kan.; Aug. 23, Jacob Davis, Green Wood, S.C.; Sept. 2, William Arkinson, McKenney, Ky.; Sept. 16, unknown negro, Centerville, Ala.; Sept. 16, Jessie Mitchell, Amelia C.H., Va.; Sept. 25, Perry Bratcher, New Boston, Tex.; Oct. 9, William Lacey, Jasper, Ala.; Oct. 22, John Gamble, Pikesville, Tenn.

OFFENSES CHARGED ARE AS FOLLOWS

Rape, 39; attempted rape, 8; alleged rape, 4; suspicion of rape, 1; murder, 44; alleged murder, 6; alleged complicity in murder, 4; murderous assault, 1; attempted murder, 1; attempted robbery, 4; arson, 4; incendiarism, 3; alleged stock poisoning, 1; poisoning wells, 2; alleged poisoning wells, 5; burglary, 1; wife beating, 1; self-defense, 1; suspected robbery, 1; assault and battery, 1; insulting whites, 2; malpractice, 1; alleged barn burning, 4; stealing, 2; unknown offense, 4; no offense, 1; race prejudice, 4; total, 159.

LYNCHINGS BY STATES

Alabama, 25; Arkansas, 7; Florida, 7; Georgia, 24; Indian Territory, 1; Illinois, 3; Kansas, 2; Kentucky, 8; Louisiana, 18; Mississippi, 17; Missouri, 3; New York, 1; South Carolina, 15; Tennessee, 10; Texas, 8; Virginia, 10.

RECORD FOR THE YEAR 1892

While it is intended that the record here presented shall include specially the lynchings of 1893, it will not be amiss to give the record for the year preceding. The facts contended for will always appear manifest—that not one-third of the victims lynched were charged with rape, and further that the charges made embraced a range of offenses from murders to misdemeanors.

In 1892 there were 241 persons lynched. The entire number is divided among the following states:

Alabama, 22; Arkansas, 25; California, 3; Florida, 11; Georgia, 17; Idaho, 8; Illinois, 1; Kansas, 3; Kentucky, 9; Louisiana, 29; Maryland, 1; Mississippi, 16; Missouri, 6; Montana, 4; New York, 1; North Carolina, 5; North Dakota, 1; Ohio, 3; South Carolina, 5; Tennessee, 28; Texas, 15; Virginia, 7; West Virginia, 5; Wyoming, 9; Arizona Territory, 3; Oklahoma, 2.

Of this number 160 were of Negro descent. Four of them were lynched in New York, Ohio and Kansas; the remainder were murdered in the South. Five of this number were females. The charges for which they were lynched cover a wide range. They are as follows:

Rape, 46; murder, 58; rioting, 3; race prejudice, 6; no cause given, 4; incendiarism, 6; robbery, 6; assault and battery, 1; attempted rape, 11; suspected robbery, 4; larceny, 1; self-defense, 1; insulting women, 2; desperadoes, 6; fraud, 1; attempted murder, 2; no offense stated, boy and girl, 2.

In the case of the boy and girl above referred to, their father, named Hastings, was accused of the murder of a white man; his fourteen-year-old daughter and sixteen-year-old son were hanged and their bodies filled with bullets, then the father was also lynched. This was in November, 1892, at Jonesville, Louisiana.

3

LYNCHING IMBECILES

(An Arkansas Butchery)

The only excuse which capital punishment attempts to find is upon the theory that the criminal is past the power of reformation and his life is a constant menace to the community. If, however, he is mentally unbalanced, irresponsible for his acts, there can be no more inhuman act conceived of than the wilful sacrifice of his life. So thoroughly is that principle grounded in the law, that all civilized society surrounds human life with a safeguard, which prevents the execution of a criminal who is insane, even if sane at the time of his criminal act. Should he become insane after its commission the law steps in and protects him during the period of his insanity. But Lynch Law has no such regard for human life. Assuming for itself an absolute supremacy over the law of the land, it has time and again dyed its hands in the blood of men who were imbeciles. Two or three noteworthy cases will suffice to show with what inhuman ferocity irresponsible men have been put to death by this system of injustice.

An instance occurred during the year 1892 in Arkansas, a report of which is given in full in the *Arkansas Democrat*, published at Little Rock, in that state, on the eleventh day of February of that year. The paper mentioned is perhaps one of the leading weeklies in that state and the account given in detail has every mark of a careful and conscientious investigation. The victims of this tragedy were a colored man, named Hamp Biscoe, his wife and a thirteen-year-old son. Hamp Biscoe, it appears, was a hard working, thrifty farmer, who lived near England, Arkansas, upon a small farm with his family. The investigation of the tragedy was conducted by a resident of Arkansas named R.B. Caries, a white man, who furnished the account to the *Arkansas Democrat* over his own signature. He says the original trouble which led to the lynching was a quarrel between Biscoe and a white man about a debt. About six years after Biscoe preempted his land, a white man made a demand of $100 upon him for services in showing him the land and making the sale. Biscoe denied the service and refused to pay the demand. The white man, however, brought suit, obtained judgment for the hundred dollars and Biscoe's farm was sold to pay the judgment.

The suit, judgment and subsequent legal proceedings appear to have driven Biscoe almost crazy and brooding over his wrongs he grew to be a confirmed imbecile. He would allow but few men, white or colored, to come upon his place, as he suspected every stranger to be planning to steal his farm. A week preceding the tragedy, a white man named Venable, whose farm adjoined Biscoe's, let down the fence and proceeded to drive through Biscoe's field. The latter saw him; grew very excited, cursed him and drove him from his farm with bitter oaths and violent threats. Venable went away and secured a warrant for Biscoe's arrest. This warrant was placed in the hands of a constable named John Ford, who took a colored deputy and two white men out to Biscoe's farm to make the arrest. When they arrived at the house Biscoe refused to be arrested and warned them he would shoot if they persisted in their attempt to arrest him. The warning was unheeded by Ford, who entered upon the premises, when Biscoe, true to his word, fired upon him. The load tore a part of his clothes from his body, one shot going through his arm and entering his breast. After he had fallen, Ford drew his revolver and shot Biscoe in the head and his wife through the arm. The Negro deputy then began firing and struck Biscoe in the small of the back. Ford's wound was not dangerous and in a few days he was able to be around again. Biscoe, however, was so severely shot that he was unable to stand after the firing was over.

Two other white men hearing the exchange of shots went to the rescue of the officers, forced open the door of Biscoe's cabin and arrested him, his wife and thirteen-year-old son, and took them, together with a babe at the breast, to a small frame house near the depot and put them under guard. The subsequent proceedings were briefly told by Mr. Carlee in the columns of the *Arkansas Democrat* above mentioned, from whose account the following excerpt is taken:

It was rumored here that the Negroes were to be lynched that night, but I do not think it was generally credited, as it was not believed that Ford was greatly hurt and the Negro was held to be fatally injured and crazy at that. But that night, about 8 o'clock, a party of perhaps twelve or fifteen men, a number of whom were known to the guards, came to the house and told the Negro guards they would take care of the prisoners now, and for them to leave; as they did not obey at once they were persuaded to leave with words that did not admit of delay.

The woman began to cry and said, "You intend to kill us to get our money." They told her to hush (she was heavy with child and had a child at her breast) as they intended to give her a nice present. The guards heard no more, but hastened to a Negro church near by and urged the preacher to go up and stop the mob. A few minutes after, the shooting began, perhaps about forty shots being fired. The white men then left rapidly and the Negroes went to the house. Hamp Biscoe and his wife were killed, the baby had a slight wound across the upper lip; the boy was still alive and lived until after midnight, talking rationally and telling who did the shooting.

He said when they came in and shot his father, he attempted to run out of doors and a young man shot him in the bowels and that he fell. He saw another man shoot his mother and a taller young man, whom he did not know, shoot his father. After they had killed them, the young man who had shot his mother pulled off her stockings and took $220 in currency that she had hid there. The men then came to the door where the boy was lying and one of them turned him over and put his pistol to his breast and shot him again. This is the story the dying boy told as near as I can get it. It is quite singular that the guards and those who had

conversed with him were not required to testify. The woman was known to
have the money as she had exposed it that day. She also had $36 in
silver, which the plunderer of the body did not get. The Negro was
undoubtedly insane and had been for several years. The citizens of this
community condemn the murder and have no sympathy with it. The Negro was
a well-to-do farmer, but had become crazed because he was convinced some
plot had been made to steal his land and only a few days ago declared
that he expected to die in defense of his home in a short time and he
did not care how soon. The killing of a woman with the child at her
breast and in her condition, and also a young boy, was extremely brutal.
As for Hamp Biscoe he was dangerous and should long have been confined
in the insane asylum. Such were the facts as near as I can get them and
you can use them as you see fit, but I would prefer you would suppress
the names charged by the Negroes with the killing.

Perhaps the civilized world will think, that with all these facts laid before the public, by a writer who signs his name to his communication, in a land where grand juries are sworn to investigate, where judges and juries are sworn to administer the law and sheriffs are paid to execute the decrees of the courts, and where, in fact, every instrument of civilization is supposed to work for the common good of all citizens, that this matter was duly investigated, the criminals apprehended and the punishment meted out to the murderers. But this is a mistake; nothing of the kind was done or attempted. Six months after the publication, above referred to, an investigator, writing to find out what had been done in the matter, received the following reply:

OFFICE OF
S.S. GLOVER,
SHERIFF AND COLLECTOR,
LONOKE COUNTY.

Lonoke, Ark., 9-12-1892

Geo. Washington, Esq.,
Chicago, Ill.
DEAR SIR:—The parties who killed Hamp Briscoe February the ninth, have
never been arrested. The parties are still in the county. It was done by
some of the citizens, and those who know will not tell.

S.S. GLOVER, Sheriff

Thus acts the mob with the victim of its fury, conscious that it will never be called to an account. Not only is this true, but the moral support of those who are chosen by the people to execute the law, is frequently given to the support of lawlessness and mob violence. The press and even the pulpit, in the main either by silence or open apology, have condoned and encouraged this state of anarchy.

TORTURED AND BURNED IN TEXAS

Never In the history of civilization has any Christian people stooped to such shocking brutality and indescribable barbarism as that which characterized the people of Paris, Texas, and adjacent communities on the first of February, 1893. The cause of this awful outbreak of human passion was the murder of a four-year-old child, daughter of a man named Vance. This man, Vance, had been a police officer in Paris for years, and was known to be a man of bad temper, overbearing manner and given to harshly treating the prisoners under his care. He had arrested Smith and, it is said, cruelly mistreated him. Whether or not the murder of his child was an art of fiendish revenge, it has not been shown, but many persons who know of the incident have suggested that the secret of the attack on the child lay in a desire for revenge against its father.

In the same town there lived a Negro, named Henry Smith, a well-known character, a kind of roustabout, who was generally considered a harmless, weak-minded fellow, not capable of doing any important work, but sufficiently able to do chores and odd jobs around the houses of the white people who cared to employ him. A few days before the final tragedy, this man, Smith, was accused of murdering Myrtle Vance. The crime of murder was of itself bad enough, and to prove that against Smith would have been amply sufficient in Texas to have committed him to the gallows, but the finding of the child so exasperated the father and his friends, that they at once shamefully exaggerated the facts and declared that the babe had been ruthlessly assaulted and then killed. The truth was bad enough, but the white people of the community made it a point to exaggerate every detail of the awful affair, and to inflame the public mind so that nothing less than immediate and violent death would satisfy the populace. As a matter of fact, the child was not brutally assaulted as the world has been told in excuse for the awful barbarism of that day. Persons who saw the child after its death, have stated, under the most solemn pledge to truth, that there was no evidence of such an assault as was published at that time, only a slight abrasion and discoloration was noticeable and that mostly about the neck. In spite of this fact, so eminent a man as Bishop Haygood deliberately and, it must also appear, maliciously falsified the fact by stating that the child was torn limb from limb, or to quote his own words, "First outraged with demoniacal cruelty and then taken by her heels and torn asunder in the mad wantonness of gorilla ferocity."

Nothing is farther from the truth than that statement. It is a coldblooded, deliberate, brutal falsehood which this Christian(?) Bishop uses to bolster up the infamous plea that the people of Paris were driven to insanity by learning that the little child had been viciously assaulted, choked to death, and then torn to pieces by a demon in human form. It was a brutal murder, but no more brutal than hundreds of murders which occur in this country, and which have been equalled every year in fiendishness and brutality, and for which the death penalty is prescribed by law and inflicted only after the person has been legally adjudged guilty of the crime. Those who knew Smith, believe that Vance had at some time given him cause to seek revenge and that this fearful crime was the outgrowth of his attempt to avenge himself of some real or fancied wrong. That the murderer was known as an imbecile, had no effect whatever upon the people who thirsted for his blood. They determined to make an example of him and proceeded to carry out their purpose with unspeakably greater ferocity than that which characterized the half-crazy object of their revenge.

For a day or so after the child was found in the woods, Smith remained in the vicinity as if nothing had happened, and when finally becoming aware that he was suspected, he made an attempt to escape. He was apprehended, however, not far from the scene of his crime and the news flashed across the country that the white Christian people of Paris, Texas and the communities thereabout had deliberately determined to lay aside all forms of law and inaugurate an entirely new form of punishment for the murder. They absolutely refused to make any inquiry as to the sanity or insanity of their prisoner, but set the day and hour when in the presence of assembled thousands they put their helpless victim to the stake, tortured him, and then burned him to death for the delectation and satisfaction of Christian people.

Lest it might be charged that any description of the deeds of that day are exaggerated, a white man's description which was published in the white journals of this country is used. The *New York Sun* of February 2, 1893, contains an account, from which we make the following excerpt:

PARIS, Tex., Feb. 1, 1893.—Henry Smith, the negro ravisher of four-year-old Myrtle Vance, has expiated in part his awful crime by death at the stake. Ever since the perpetration of his awful crime this city and the entire surrounding country has been in a wild frenzy of excitement. When the news came last night that he had been captured at Hope, Ark., that he had been identified by B.B. Sturgeon, James T. Hicks, and many other of the Paris searching party, the city was wild with joy over the apprehension of the brute. Hundreds of people poured into the city from the adjoining country and the word passed from lip to lip that the punishment of the fiend should fit the crime that death by fire was the penalty Smith should pay for the most atrocious murder and terrible outrage in Texas history. Curious and sympathizing alike, they came on train and wagons, on horse, and on foot to see if the frail mind of a man could think of a way to sufficiently punish the perpetrator of so terrible a crime. Whisky shops were closed, unruly mobs were dispersed, schools were dismissed by a proclamation from the mayor, and everything was done in a business-like manner.

MEETING OF CITIZENS

About 2 o'clock Friday a mass meeting was called at the courthouse and captains appointed to search for the child. She was found mangled beyond recognition, covered with leaves and brush as above mentioned. As soon as it was learned upon the recovery of the body that the crime was so atrocious the whole town turned out in the chase. The railroads put up bulletins offering free transportation to all who would join in the search. Posses went in every direction, and not a stone was left unturned. Smith was tracked to Detroit on foot, where he jumped on a freight train and left for his old home in Hempstead county, Arkansas. To this county he was tracked and yesterday captured at Clow, a flag station on the Arkansas & Louisiana railway about twenty miles north of Hope. Upon being questioned the fiend denied everything, but upon being stripped for examination his undergarments were seen to be spattered with blood and a part of his shirt was torn off. He was kept under heavy guard at Hope last night, and later on confessed the crime.

This morning he was brought through Texarkana, where 5,000 people awaited the train, anxious to see a man who had received the fate of Ed. Coy. At that place speeches were made by prominent Paris citizens, who asked that the prisoner be not molested by Texarkana people, but that the guard be allowed to deliver him up to the outraged and indignant citizens of Paris. Along the road the train gathered strength from the various towns, the people crowded upon the platforms and tops of coaches anxious to see the lynching and the negro who was soon to be delivered to an infuriated mob.

BURNED AT THE STAKE

Arriving here at 12 o'clock the train was met by a surging mass of humanity 10,000 strong. The negro was placed upon a carnival float in mockery of a king upon his throne, and, followed by an immense crowd, was escorted through the city so that all might see the most inhuman monster known in current history. The line of march was up Main Street to the square, around the square down Clarksville street to Church Street, thence to the open prairies about 300 yards from the Texas & Pacific depot. Here Smith was placed upon a scaffold, six feet square and ten feet high, securely bound, within the view of all beholders. Here the victim was tortured for fifty minutes by red-hot iron brands thrust against his quivering body. Commencing at the feet the brands were placed against him inch by inch until they were thrust against the face. Then, being apparently dead, kerosene was poured upon him, cottonseed hulls placed beneath him and set on fire. In less time than it takes to relate it, the tortured man was wafted beyond the grave to another fire, hotter and more terrible than the one just experienced.

Curiosity seekers have carried away already all that was left of the memorable event, even to pieces of charcoal. The cause of the crime was that Henry Vance when a deputy policeman, in the course of his duty was called to arrest Henry Smith for being drunk and disorderly. The Negro was unruly, and Vance was forced to use his club. The Negro swore vengeance, and several times assaulted

Vance. In his greed for revenge, last Thursday, he grabbed up the little girl and committed the crime. The father is prostrated with grief and the mother now lies at death's door, but she has lived to see the slayer of her innocent babe suffer the most horrible death that could be conceived.

TORTURE BEYOND DESCRIPTION

Words to describe the awful torture inflicted upon Smith cannot be found. The Negro, for a long time after starting on the journey to Paris, did not realize his plight. At last when he was told that he must die by slow torture he begged for protection. His agony was awful. He pleaded and writhed in bodily and mental pain. Scarcely had the train reached Paris than this torture commenced. His clothes were torn off piecemeal and scattered in the crowd, people catching the shreds and putting them away as mementos. The child's father, her brother, and two uncles then gathered about the Negro as he lay fastened to the torture platform and thrust hot irons into his quivering flesh. It was horrible—the man dying by slow torture in the midst of smoke from his own burning flesh. Every groan from the fiend, every contortion of his body was cheered by the thickly packed crowd of 10,000 persons. The mass of beings 600 yards in diameter, the scaffold being the center. After burning the feet and legs, the hot irons—plenty of fresh ones being at hand—were rolled up and down Smith's stomach, back, and arms. Then the eyes were burned out and irons were thrust down his throat.

The men of the Vance family having wreaked vengeance, the crowd piled all kinds of combustible stuff around the scaffold, poured oil on it and set it afire. The Negro rolled and tossed out of the mass, only to be pushed back by the people nearest him. He tossed out again, and was roped and pulled back. Hundreds of people turned away, but the vast crowd still looked calmly on. People were here from every part of this section. They came from Dallas, Fort Worth, Sherman, Denison, Bonham, Texarkana, Fort Smith, Ark., and a party of fifteen came from Hempstead county, Arkansas, where he was captured. Every train that came in was loaded to its utmost capacity, and there were demands at many points for special trains to bring the people here to see the unparalleled punishment for an unparalleled crime. When the news of the burning went over the country like wildfire, at every country town anvils boomed forth the announcement.

SHOULD HAVE BEEN IN AN ASYLUM

It may not be amiss in connection with this awful affair, in proof of our assertion that Smith was an imbecile, to give the testimony of a well-known colored minister, who lived at Paris, Texas, at the time of the lynching. He was a witness of the awful scenes there enacted, and attempted, in the name of God and humanity, to interfere in the programme. He barely escaped with his life, was driven out of the city and became an exile because of his actions. Reverend King was in New York about the middle of February, and he was there interviewed for a daily paper for that city, and we quote his account as an eye witness of the affair. Said he:

I was ridden out of Paris on a rail because I was the only man in Lamar county to raise my voice against the lynching of Smith. I opposed the illegal measures before the arrival of Henry Smith as a prisoner, and I was warned that I might meet his fate if I was not careful; but the sense of justice made me bold, and when I saw the poor wretch trembling with fear, and got so near him that I could hear his teeth chatter, I determined to stand by him to the last.

I hated him for his crime, but two crimes do not make a virtue; and in the brief conversation I had with Smith I was more firmly convinced than ever that he was irresponsible.

I had known Smith for years, and there were times when Smith was out of his head for weeks. Two years ago I made an effort to have him put in an asylum, but the white people were trying to fasten the murder of a young colored girl upon him, and would not listen. For days before the murder of the little Vance girl, Smith was out of his head and dangerous. He had just undergone an attack of delirium tremens and was in no condition to be allowed at large. He realized his condition, for I spoke with him not three weeks ago, and in answer to my exhortations, he promised to reform. The next time I saw him was on the day of his execution.

"Drink did it! drink did it," he sobbed. Then bowing his face in his hands, he asked: "Is it true, did I kill her? Oh, my God, my God!" For a moment he seemed to forget the awful fate that awaited him, and his body swayed to and fro with grief. Some one seized me by the shoulder and hurled me back, and Smith fell writhing to the ground in terror as four men seized his arms to drag him to the float on which he was to be exhibited before he was finally burned at the stake.

I followed the procession and wept aloud as I saw little children of my own race follow the unfortunate man and taunt him with jeers. Even at the stake, children of both sexes and colors gathered in groups, and when the father of the murdered child raised the hissing iron with which he was about to torture the helpless victim, the children became as frantic as the grown people and struggled forward to obtain places of advantage.

It was terrible. One little tot scarcely older than little Myrtle Vance clapped her baby hands as her father held her on his shoulders above the heads of the people.

"For God's sake," I shouted, "send the children home."
"No, no," shouted a hundred maddened voices; "let them learn a lesson."

I love children, but as I looked about the little faces distorted with
passion and the bloodshot eyes of the cruel parents who held them high
in their arms, I thanked God that I have none of my own.

As the hot iron sank deep into poor Henry's flesh a hideous yell rent
the air, and, with a sound as terrible as the cry, of lost souls on
judgment day, 20,000 maddened people took up the victim's cry of agony
and a prolonged howl of maddened glee rent the air.

No one was himself now. Every man, woman and child in that awful crowd
was worked up to a greater frenzy than that which actuated Smith's
horrible crime. The people were capable of any new atrocity now, and as
Smith's yells became more and more frequent, it was difficult to hold
the crowd back, so anxious were the savages to participate in the
sickening tortures.

For half an hour I tried to pray as the beads of agony rolled down my
forehead and bathed my face.

For an instant a hush spread over the people. I could stand no more, and
with a superhuman effort dashed through the compact mass of humanity and
stood at the foot of the burning scaffold.

"In the name of God," I cried, "I command you to cease this torture."

The heavy butt of a Winchester rifle descended on my head and I fell to
the ground. Rough hands seized me and angry men bore me away, and I was
thankful.

At the outskirts of the crowd I was attacked again, and then several
men, no doubt glad to get away from the fearful place, escorted me to my
home, where I was allowed to take a small amount of clothing. A jeering
crowd gathered without, and when I appeared at the door ready hands
seized me and I was placed upon a rail, and, with curses and oaths,
taken to the railway station and placed upon a train. As the train moved
out some one thrust a roll of bills into my hand and said, "God bless
you, but it was no use."

When asked if he should ever return to Paris, Mr. King said: "I shall never go
south again. The impressions of that awful day will stay with me forever."

LYNCHING OF INNOCENT MEN

(Lynched on Account of Relationship)

If no other reason appealed to the sober sense of the American people to check the growth of Lynch Law, the absolute unreliability and recklessness of the mob in inflicting punishment for crimes done, should do so. Several instances of this spirit have occurred in the year past. In Louisiana, near New Orleans, in July, 1893, Roselius Julian, a colored man, shot and killed a white judge, named Victor Estopinal. The cause of the shooting has never been definitely ascertained. It is claimed that the Negro resented an insult to his wife, and the killing of the white man was an act of a Negro (who dared) to defend his home. The judge was killed in the court house, and Julian, heavily armed, made his escape to the swamps near the city. He has never been apprehended, nor has any information ever been gleaned as to his whereabouts. A mob determined to secure the fugitive murderer and burn him alive. The swamps were hunted through and through in vain, when, being unable to wreak their revenge upon the murderer, the mob turned its attention to his unfortunate relatives. Dispatches from New Orleans, dated September 19, 1893, described the affair as follows:

Posses were immediately organized and the surrounding country was scoured, but the search was fruitless so far as the real criminal was concerned. The mother, three brothers and two sisters of the Negro were arrested yesterday at the Black Ridge in the rear of the city by the police and taken to the little jail on Judge Estopinal's place about Southport, because of the belief that they were succoring the fugitive.

About 11 o'clock twenty-five men, some armed with rifles and shotguns, came up to the jail. They unlocked the door and held a conference among themselves as to what they should do. Some were in favor of hanging the five, while others insisted that only two of the brothers should be strung up. This was finally agreed to, and the two doomed negroes were hurried to a pasture one hundred yards distant, and there asked to take their last chance of saving their lives by making a confession, but the Negroes made no reply. They were then told to kneel down and pray. One did so, the other remained standing, but both prayed fervently. The taller Negro was then hoisted up. The shorter Negro stood gazing at the horrible death of his brother without flinching. Five minutes later he was also hanged. The mob decided to take the remaining brother out to Camp Parapet and hang him there. The other two were to be taken out and flogged, with an order to get out of the parish in less than half an hour. The third brother, Paul, was taken out to the camp, which is about a mile distant in the interior, and there he was hanged to a tree.

Another young man, who was in no way related to Julian, who perhaps did not even know the man and who was entirely innocent of any offense in connection therewith, was murdered by the same mob. The same paper says:

> During the search for Julian on Saturday one branch of the posse visited
> the house of a Negro family in the neighborhood of Camp Parapet, and
> failing to find the object of their search, tried to induce John Willis,
> a young Negro, to disclose the whereabouts of Julian. He refused to do
> so, or could not do so, and was kicked to death by the gang.

AN INDIANA CASE

Almost equal to the ferocity of the mob which killed the three brothers, Julian and the unoffending, John Willis, because of the murder of Judge Estopinal, was the action of a mob near Vincennes, Ind. In this case a wealthy colored man, named Allen Butler, who was well known in the community, and enjoyed the confidence and respect of the entire country, was made the victim of a mob and hung because his son had become unduly intimate with a white girl who was a servant around his house. There was no pretense that the facts were otherwise than as here stated. The woman lived at Butler's house as a servant, and she and Butler's son fell in love with each other, and later it was found that the girl was in a delicate condition. It was claimed, but with how much truth no one has ever been able to tell, that the father had procured an abortion, or himself had operated on the girl, and that she had left the house to go back to her home. It was never claimed that the father was in any way responsible for the action of his son, but the authorities procured the arrest of both father and son, and at the preliminary examination the father gave bail to appear before the Grand Jury when it should convene. On the same night, however, the mob took the matter in hand and with the intention of hanging the son. It assembled near Sumner, while the boy, who had been unable to give bail, was lodged in jail at Lawrenceville. As it was impossible to reach Lawrenceville and hang the son, the leaders of the mob concluded they would go to Butler's house and hang him. Butler was found at his home, taken out by the mob and hung to a tree. This was in the lawabiding state of Indiana, which furnished the United States its last president and which claims all the honor, pride and glory of northern civilization. None of the leaders of the mob were apprehended, and no steps whatever were taken to bring the murderers to justice.

KILLED FOR HIS STEPFATHER'S CRIME

An account has been given of the cremation of Henry Smith, at Paris, Texas, for the murder of the infant child of a man named Vance. It would appear that human ferocity was not sated when it vented itself upon a human being by burning his eyes out, by thrusting a red-hot iron down his throat, and then by burning his body to ashes. Henry Smith, the victim of these savage orgies, was beyond all the power of torture, but a few miles outside of Paris, some members of the community concluded that it would be proper to kill a stepson named William Butler as a partial penalty for the original crime. This young man, against whom no word has ever been said, and who was in fact an orderly, peaceable boy, had been watched with the severest scrutiny by members of the mob who believed he knew something of the whereabouts of Smith. He declared from the very first that he did not know where his stepfather was, which statement was well proven to be a fact after the discovery of Smith in Arkansas, whence he had fled through swamps and woods and unfrequented places. Yet Butler was apprehended, placed under arrest, and on the night of February 6, taken out on Hickory Creek, five miles southeast of Paris, and hung for his stepfather's crime. After his body was suspended in the air, the mob filled it with bullets.

LYNCHED BECAUSE THE JURY ACQUITTED HIM

The entire system of the judiciary of this country is in the hands of white people. To this add the fact of the inherent prejudice against colored people, and it will be clearly seen that a white jury is certain to find a Negro prisoner guilty if there is the least evidence to warrant such a finding.

Meredith Lewis was arrested in Roseland, La., in July of last year. A white jury found him not guilty of the crime of murder wherewith he stood charged. This did not suit the mob. A few nights after the verdict was rendered, and he declared to be innocent, a mob gathered in his vicinity and went to his house. He was called, and suspecting nothing, went outside. He was seized and hurried off to a convenient spot and hanged by the neck until he was dead for the murder of a woman of which the jury had said he was innocent.

LYNCHED AS A SCAPEGOAT

Wednesday, July 5, about 10 o'clock in the morning, a terrible crime was committed within four miles of Wickliffe, Ky. Two girls, Mary and Ruby Ray, were found murdered a short distance from their home. The news of this terrible cowardly murder of two helpless young girls spread like wild fire, and searching parties scoured the territory surrounding Wickliffe and Bardwell. Two of the searching party, the Clark brothers, saw a man enter the Dupoyster cornfield; they got their guns and fired at the fleeing figure, but without effect; he got away, but they said he was a white man or nearly so. The search continued all day without effect, save the arrest of two or three strange Negroes. A bloodhound was brought from the penitentiary and put on the trail which he followed from the scene of the murder to the river and into the boat of a fisherman named Gordon. Gordon stated that he had ferried one man and only one across the river about about half past six the evening of July 5; that his passenger sat in front of him, and he was a white man or a very bright mulatto, who could not be told from a white man. The bloodhound was put across the river in the boat, and he struck a trail again at Bird's Point on the Missouri side, ran about three hundred yards to the cottage of a white farmer named Grant and there lay down refusing to go further.

Thursday morning a brakesman on a freight train going out of Sikeston, Mo., discovered a Negro stealing a ride; he ordered him off and had hot words which terminated in a fight. The brakesman had the Negro arrested. When arrested, between 11 and 12 o'clock, he had on a dark woolen shirt, light pants and coat, and no vest. He had twelve dollars in paper, two silver dollars and ninety-five cents in change; he had also four rings in his pockets, a knife and a razor which were rusted and stained. The Sikeston authorities immediately jumped to the conclusion that this man was the murderer for whom the Kentuckians across the river were searching. They telegraphed to Bardwell that their prisoner had on no coat, but wore a blue vest and pants which would perhaps correspond with the coat found at the scene of the murder, and that the names of the murdered girls were in the rings found in his possession.

As soon as this news was received, the sheriffs of Ballard and Carlisle counties and a posse(?) of thirty well-armed and determined Kentuckians, who had pledged their word the prisoner should be taken back to the scene of the supposed crime, to be executed there if proved to be the guilty man, chartered a train and at nine o'clock Thursday night started for Sikeston. Arriving there two hours later, the sheriff at Sikeston, who had no warrant for the prisoner's arrest and detention, delivered him into the hands of the mob without authority for so doing, and accompanied them to Bird's Point. The prisoner gave his name as Miller, his home at Springfield, and said he had never been in Kentucky in his life, but the sheriff turned him over to the mob to be taken to Wickliffe, that Frank Gordon, the fisherman, who had put a man across the river might identify him.

In other words, the protection of the law was withdrawn from C.J. Miller, and he was given to a mob by this sheriff at Sikeston, who knew that the prisoner's life depended on one man's word. After an altercation with the train men, who wanted another $50 for taking the train back to Bird's Point, the crowd arrived there at three o'clock, Friday morning. Here was anchored *The Three States*, a ferryboat plying between Wickliffe, Ky, Cairo, Ill., and Bird's Point, Mo. This boat left Cairo at twelve o'clock, Thursday, with nearly three hundred of Cairo's best(?) citizens and thirty kegs of beer on board. This was consumed while the crowd and the bloodhound waited for the prisoner.

When the prisoner was on board *The Three States* the dog was turned loose, and after moving aimlessly around, followed the crowd to where Miller sat handcuffed and there stopped. The crowd closed in on the pair and insisted that the brute had identified him because of that action. When the boat reached Wickliffe, Gordon, the fisherman, was called on to say whether the prisoner was the man he ferried over the river the day of the murder.

[Illustration: Lynching of C.J. Miller, at Bardwell, Kentucky, July 7, 1893.]

The sheriff of Ballard County informed him, sternly that if the prisoner was not the man, he (the fisherman) would be held responsible as knowing who the guilty man was. Gordon stated before, that the man he ferried across was a white man or a bright colored man; Miller was a dark brown skinned man, with kinky hair, "neither yellow nor black," says the *Cairo Evening Telegram* of Friday, July 7. The fisherman went up to Miller from behind, looked at him without speaking for fully five minutes, then slowly said, "Yes, that's the man I crossed over." This was about six o'clock, Friday morning, and the crowd wished to hang Miller then and there. But Mr. Ray, the father of the girls, insisted that he be taken to Bardwell, the county seat of Ballard, and twelve miles inland. He said he thought a white man committed the crime, and that he was not satisfied that was the man. They took him to Bardwell and at ten o'clock, this same excited, unauthorized mob undertook to determine Miller's guilt. One of the Clark brothers who shot at a fleeing man in the Dupoyster cornfield, said the prisoner was the same man; the other said he was not, but the testimony of the first was accepted. A colored woman who had said she gave breakfast to a colored man clad in a blue flannel suit the morning of the murder, said positively that she had never seen Miller before. The gold rings found in his possession had no names in them, as had been asserted, and Mr. Ray said they did not belong to his daughters. Meantime a funeral pyre for the purpose of burning Miller to death had been erected in the center of the village. While the crowd swayed by passion was clamoring that he be burnt, Miller stepped forward and made the following statement: "My name is C.J. Miller. I am from Springfield, Ill.; my wife lives at 716 N. 2d Street. I am here among you today, looked upon as one of the most brutal men before the people. I stand here surrounded by men who are excited, men who are not willing to let the law take its course, and as far as the crime is concerned, I have committed no crime, and certainly no crime gross enough to deprive me of my life and liberty to walk upon the green earth."

A telegram was sent to the chief of the police at Springfield, Ill., asking if one C.J. Miller lived there. An answer in the negative was returned. A few hours after, it was ascertained that a man named Miller, and his wife, did live at the number the prisoner gave in his speech, but the information came to Bardwell too late to do the prisoner any good. Miller was taken to jail, every stitch of clothing literally torn from his body and examined again. On the lower left side of the bosom of his shirt was found a dark reddish spot about the size of a dime. Miller said it was paint which he had gotten on him at Jefferson Barracks. This spot was only on the right side, and could not be seen from the under side at all, thus showing it had not gone through the cloth as blood or any liquid substance would do.

Chief-of-Police Mahaney, of Cairo, Ill., was with the prisoner, and he took his knife and scraped at the spot, particles of which came off in his hand. Miller told them to take his clothes to any expert, and if the spot was shown to be blood, they might do anything they wished with him. They took his clothes away and were gone some time. After a while they were brought back and thrown into the cell without a word. It is needless to say that if the spot had been found to be blood, that fact would have been announced, and the shirt retained as evidence. Meanwhile numbers of rough, drunken men crowded into the cell and tried to force a confession of the deed from the prisoner's lips. He refused to talk save to reiterate his innocence. To Mr. Mahaney, who talked seriously and kindly to him, telling him the mob meant to burn and torture him at three o'clock, Miller said: "Burning and torture here lasts but a little while, but if I die with a lie on my soul, I shall be tortured forever. I am innocent." For more than three hours, all sorts of pressure in the way of threats, abuse and urging, was brought to bear to force him to confess to the murder and thus justify the mob in its deed of murder. Miller remained firm; but as the hour drew near, and the crowd became more impatient, he asked for a priest. As none could be procured, he then asked for a Methodist minister, who came, prayed with the doomed man, baptized him and exhorted Miller to confess. To keep up the flagging spirits of the dense crowd around the jail, the rumor went out more than once, that Miller had confessed. But the solemn assurance of the minister, chief-of-police, and leading editor—who were with Miller all along—is that this rumor is absolutely false.

At three o'clock the mob rushed to the jail to secure the prisoner. Mr. Ray had changed his mind about the promised burning; he was still in doubt as to the prisoner's guilt. He again addressed the crowd to that effect, urging them not to burn Miller, and the mob heeded him so far, that they compromised on hanging instead of burning, which was agreed to by Mr. Ray. There was a loud yell, and a rush was made for the prisoner. He was stripped naked, his clothing literally torn from his body, and his shirt was tied around his loins. Some one declared the rope was a "white man's death," and a log-chain, nearly a hundred feet in length, weighing over one hundred pounds, was placed round Miller's neck and body, and he was led and dragged through the streets of the village in that condition followed by thousands of people. He fainted from exhaustion several times, but was supported to the platform where they first intended burning him.

The chain was hooked around his neck, a man climbed the telegraph pole and the other end of the chain was passed up to him and made fast to the cross-arm. Others brought a long forked stick which Miller was made to straddle. By this means he was raised several feet from the ground and then let fall. The first fall broke his neck, but he was raised in this way and let fall a second time. Numberless shots were fired into the dangling body, for most of that crowd were heavily armed, and had been drinking all day.

Miller's body hung thus exposed from three to five o'clock, during which time, several photographs of him as he hung dangling at the end of the chain were taken, and his toes and fingers were cut off. His body was taken down, placed on the platform, the torch applied, and in a few moments there was nothing left of C.J. Miller save a few bones and ashes. Thus perished another of the many victims of Lynch Law, but it is the honest and sober belief of many who witnessed the scene that an innocent man has been barbarously and shockingly put to death in the glare of the nineteenth-century civilization, by those who profess to believe in Christianity, law and order.

5

LYNCHED FOR ANYTHING OR NOTHING

(Lynched for Wife Beating)
In nearly all communities wife beating is punishable with a fine, and in no community is it made a felony. Dave Jackson, of Abita, La., was a colored man who had beaten his wife. He had not killed her, nor seriously wounded her, but as Louisiana lynchers had not filled out their quota of crimes, his case was deemed of sufficient importance to apply the method of that barbarous people. He was in the custody of the officials, but the mob went to the jail and took him out in front of the prison and hanged him by the neck until he was dead. This was in Nov. 1893.

HANGED FOR STEALING HOGS

Details are very meagre of a lynching which occurred near Knox Point, La., on the twenty-fourth of October, 1893. Upon one point, however, there was no uncertainty, and that is, that the persons lynched were Negroes. It was claimed that they had been stealing hogs, but even this claim had not been subjected to the investigation of a court. That matter was not considered necessary. A few of the neighbors who had lost hogs suspected these men were responsible for their loss, and made up their minds to furnish an example for others to be warned by. The two men were secured by a mob and hanged.

LYNCHED FOR NO OFFENSE

Perhaps the most characteristic feature of this record of lynch law for the year 1893, is the remarkable fact that five human beings were lynched and that the matter was considered of so little importance that the powerful press bureaus of the country did not consider the matter of enough importance to ascertain the causes for which they were hanged. It tells the world, with perhaps greater emphasis than any other feature of the record, that Lynch Law has become so common in the United States that the finding of the dead body of a Negro, suspended between heaven and earth to the limb of a tree, is of so slight importance that neither the civil authorities nor press agencies consider the matter worth investigating. July 21, in Shelby County, Tenn., a colored man by the name of Charles Martin was lynched. July 30, at Paris, Mo., a colored man named William Steen shared the same fate. December 28, Mack Segars was announced to have been lynched at Brantley, Alabama. August 31, at Yarborough, Texas, and on September 19, at Houston, a colored man was found lynched, but so little attention was paid to the matter that not only was no record made as to why these last two men were lynched, but even their names were not given. The dispatches simply stated that an unknown Negro was found lynched in each case.

There are friends of humanity who feel their souls shrink from any compromise with murder, but whose deep and abiding reverence for womanhood causes them to hesitate in giving their support to this crusade against Lynch Law, out of fear that they may encourage the miscreants whose deeds are worse than murder. But to these friends it must appear certain that these five men could not have been guilty of any terrible crime. They were simply lynched by parties of men who had it in their power to kill them, and who chose to avenge some fancied wrong by murder, rather than submit their grievances to court.

LYNCHED BECAUSE THEY WERE SAUCY

At Moberly, Mo., February 18 and at Fort Madison, S.C., June 2, both in 1892, a record was made in the line of lynching which should certainly appeal to every humanitarian who has any regard for the sacredness of human life. John Hughes, of Moberly, and Isaac Lincoln, of Fort Madison, and Will Lewis in Tullahoma, Tenn., suffered death for no more serious charge than that they "were saucy to white people." In the days of slavery it was held to be a very serious matter for a colored person to fail to yield the sidewalk at the demand of a white person, and it will not be surprising to find some evidence of this intolerance existing in the days of freedom. But the most that could be expected as a penalty for acting or speaking saucily to a white person would be a slight physical chastisement to make the Negro "know his place" or an arrest and fine. But Missouri, Tennessee and South Carolina chose to make precedents in their cases and as a result both men, after being charged with their offense and apprehended, were taken by a mob and lynched. The civil authorities, who in either case would have been very quick to satisfy the aggrieved white people had they complained and brought the prisoners to court, by imposing proper penalty upon them, did not feel it their duty to make any investigation after the Negroes were killed. They were dead and out of the way and as no one would be called upon to render an account for their taking off, the matter was dismissed from the public mind.

LYNCHED FOR A QUARREL

One of the most notable instances of lynching for the year 1893, occurred about the twentieth of September. It was notable for the fact that the mayor of the city exerted every available power to protect the victim of the lynching from the mob. In his splendid endeavor to uphold the law, the mayor called out the troops, and the result was a deadly fight between the militia and mob, nine of the mob being killed. The trouble occurred at Roanoke, Va. It is frequently claimed that lynchings occur only in sparsely settled districts, and, in fact, it is a favorite plea of governors and reverend apologists to couple two arrant falsehoods, stating that lynchings occur only because of assaults upon white women, and that these assaults occur and the lynchings follow in thinly inhabited districts where the power of the law is entirely inadequate to meet the emergency. This Roanoke case is a double refutation, for it not only disproves the alleged charge that the Negro assaulted a white woman, as was telegraphed all over the country at the time, but it also shows conclusively that even in one of the largest cities of the old state of Virginia, one of the original thirteen colonies, which prides itself of being the mother of presidents, it was possible for a lynching to occur in broad daylight under circumstances of revolting savagery.

When the news first came from Roanoke of the contemplated lynching, it was stated that a big burly Negro had assaulted a white woman, that he had been apprehended and that the citizens were determined to summarily dispose of his case. Mayor Trout was a man who believed in maintaining the majesty of the law, and who at once gave notice that no lynching would be permitted in Roanoke, and that the Negro, whose name was Smith, being in the custody of the law, should be dealt with according to law; but the mob did not pay any attention to the brave words of the mayor. It evidently thought that it was only another case of swagger, such as frequently characterizes lynching episodes. Mayor Trout, finding immense crowds gathering about the city, and fearing an attempt to lynch Smith, called out the militia and stationed them at the jail.

It was known that the woman refused to accuse Smith of assaulting her, and that his offense consisted in quarreling with her about the change of money in a transaction in which he bought something from her market booth. Both parties lost their temper, and the result was a row from which Smith had to make his escape. At once the old cry was sounded that the woman had been assaulted, and in a few hours all the town was wild with people thirsting for the assailant's blood. The further incidents of that day may well be told by a dispatch from Roanoke under date of the twenty-first of September and published in the *Chicago Record*. It says:

It is claimed by members of the military company that they frequently warned the mob to keep away from the jail, under penalty of being shot. Capt. Bird told them he was under orders to protect the prisoner whose life the mob so eagerly sought, and come what may he would not allow him to be taken by the mob. To this the crowd replied with hoots and derisive jeers. The rioters appeared to become frenzied at the determined stand taken by the men and Captain Bird, and finally a crowd of excited men made a rush for the side door of the jail. The captain directed his men to drive the would-be lynchers back.

At this moment the mob opened fire on the soldiers. This appeared for a moment to startle the captain and his men. But it was only for a moment. Then he coolly gave the command: "Ready! aim! fire!" The company obeyed to the instant, and poured a volley of bullets into that part of the mob which was trying to batter down the side door of the jail.

The rioters fell back before the fire of the militia, leaving one man writhing in the agonies of death at the doorstep. There was a lull for a moment. Then the word was quickly passed through the throng in front of the jail and down the street that a man was killed. Then there was an awful rush toward the little band of soldiers. Excited men were yelling like demons.

The fight became general, and ere it was ended nine men were dead and more than forty wounded.

This stubborn stand on behalf of law and order disconcerted the crowd and it fell back in disorder. It did not long remain inactive but assembled again for a second assault. Having only a small band of militia, and knowing they would be absolutely at the mercy of the thousands who were gathering to wreak vengeance upon them, the mayor ordered them to disperse and go to their homes, and he himself, having been wounded, was quietly conveyed out of the city.

The next day the mob grew in numbers and its rage increased in its intensity. There was no longer any doubt that Smith, innocent as he was of any crime, would be killed, for with the mayor out of the city and the governor of the state using no effort to control the mob, it was only a question of a few hours when the assault would be repeated and its victim put to death. All this happened as per programme. The description of that morning's carnival appeared in the paper above quoted and reads as follows:

A squad of twenty men took the negro Smith from three policemen just before five o'clock this morning and hanged him to a hickory limb on Ninth Avenue, in the residence section of the city. They riddled his body with bullets and put a placard on it saying: "This is Mayor Trout's friend." A coroner's jury of Bismel was summoned and viewed the body and rendered a verdict of death at the hands of unknown men. Thousands of persons visited the scene of the lynching between daylight and eight o'clock when the body was cut down. After the jury had completed its work the body was placed in the hands of officers, who were unable to keep back the mob. Three hundred men tried to drag the body through the streets of the town, but the Rev. Dr. Campbell of the First Presbyterian church and Capt. R.B. Moorman, with pleas and by force prevented them.

Capt. Moorman hired a wagon and the body was put in it. It was then conveyed to the bank of the Roanoke, about two miles from the scene of the lynching. Here the body was dragged from the wagon by ropes for about 200 yards and burned. Piles of dry brushwood were brought, and the body was placed upon it, and more brushwood piled on the body, leaving only the head bare. The whole pile was then saturated with coal oil and a match was applied. The body was consumed within an hour. The cremation was witnessed by several thousand people. At one time the mob threatened to burn the Negro in Mayor Trout's yard.

Thus did the people of Roanoke, Va., add this measure of proof to maintain our contention that it is only necessary to charge a Negro with a crime in order to secure his certain death. It was well known in the city before he was killed that he had not assaulted the woman with whom he had had the trouble, but he dared to have an altercation with a white woman, and he must pay the penalty. For an offense which would not in any civilized community have brought upon him a punishment greater than a fine of a few dollars, this unfortunate Negro was hung, shot and burned.

SUSPECTED, INNOCENT AND LYNCHED

Five persons, Benjamin Jackson, his wife, Mahala Jackson, his mother-in-law, Lou Carter, Rufus Bigley, were lynched near Quincy, Miss., the charge against them being suspicion of well poisoning. It appears from the newspaper dispatches at that time that a family by the name of Woodruff was taken ill in September of 1892. As a result of their illness one or more of the family are said to have died, though that matter is not stated definitely. It was suspected that the cause of their illness was the existence of poison in the water, some miscreant having placed poison in the well. Suspicion pointed to a colored man named Benjamin Jackson who was at once arrested. With him also were arrested his wife and mother-in-law and all were held on the same charge.

The matter came up for judicial investigation, but as might have been expected, the white people concluded it was unnecessary to wait the result of the investigation—that it was preferable to hang the accused first and try him afterward. By this method of procedure, the desired result was always obtained— the accused was hanged. Accordingly Benjamin Jackson was taken from the officers by a crowd of about two hundred people, while the inquest was being held, and hanged. After the killing of Jackson, the inquest was continued to ascertain the possible connection of the other persons charged with the crime. Against the wife and mother-in-law of the unfortunate man there was not the slightest evidence and the coroner's jury was fair enough to give them their liberty. They were declared innocent and returned to their homes. But this did not protect the women from the demands of the Christian white people of that section of the country. In any other land and with any other people, the fact that these two accused persons were women would have pleaded in their favor for protection and fair play, but that had no weight with the Mississippi Christians nor the further fact that a jury of white men had declared them innocent. The hanging of one victim on an unproven charge did not begin to satisfy the mob in its bloodthirsty demands and the result was that even after the women had been discharged, they were at once taken in charge by a mob, which hung them by the neck until they were dead.

Still the mob was not satisfied. During the coroner's investigation the name of a fourth person, Rufus Bigley, was mentioned. He was acquainted with the Jacksons and that fact, together with some testimony adduced at the inquest, prompted the mob to decide that he should die also. Search was at once made for him and the next day he was apprehended. He was not given over into the hands of the civil authorities for trial nor did the coroner's inquest find that he was guilty, but the mob was quite sufficient in itself. After finding Bigley, he was strung up to a tree and his body left hanging, where it was found next day. It may be remarked here in passing that this instance of the moral degradation of the people of Mississippi did not excite any interest in the public at large. American Christianity heard of this awful affair and read of its details and neither press nor pulpit gave the matter more than a passing comment. Had it occurred in the wilds of interior Africa, there would have been an outcry from the humane people of this country against the savagery which would so mercilessly put men and women to death. But it was an evidence of American civilization to be passed by unnoticed, to be denied or condoned as the requirements of any future emergency might determine.

LYNCHED FOR AN ATTEMPTED ASSAULT

With only a little more aggravation than that of Smith who quarreled at Roanoke with the market woman, was the assault which operated as the incentive to a most brutal lynching in Memphis, Tenn. Memphis is one of the queen cities of the south, with a population of about seventy thousand souls—easily one of the twenty largest, most progressive and wealthiest cities of the United States. And yet in its streets there occurred a scene of shocking savagery which would have disgraced the Congo. No woman was harmed, no serious indignity suffered. Two women driving to town in a wagon, were suddenly accosted by Lee Walker. He claimed that he demanded something to eat. The women claimed that he attempted to assault them. They gave such an alarm that he ran away. At once the dispatches spread over the entire country that a big, burly Negro had brutally assaulted two women. Crowds began to search for the alleged fiend. While hunting him they shot another Negro dead in his tracks for refusing to stop when ordered to do so. After a few days Lee Walker was found, and put in jail in Memphis until the mob there was ready for him.

The *Memphis Commercial* of Sunday, July 23, contains a full account of the tragedy from which the following extracts are made:

At 12 o'clock last night, Lee Walker, who attempted to outrage Miss Mollie McCadden, last Tuesday morning, was taken from the county jail and hanged to a telegraph pole just north of the prison. All day rumors were afloat that with nightfall an attack would be made upon the jail, and as everyone anticipated that a vigorous resistance would be made, a conflict between the mob and the authorities was feared.

At 10 o'clock Capt. O'Haver, Sergt. Horan and several patrolmen were on hand, but they could do nothing with the crowd. An attack by the mob was made on the door in the south wall, and it yielded. Sheriff McLendon and several of his men threw themselves into the breach, but two or three of the storming party shoved by. They were seized by the police, but were not subdued, the officers refraining from using their clubs. The entire mob might at first have been dispersed by ten policemen who would use their clubs, but the sheriff insisted that no violence be done.

The mob got an iron rail and used it as a battering ram against the lobby doors. Sheriff McLendon tried to stop them, and some one of the mob knocked him down with a chair. Still he counseled moderation and would not order his deputies and the police to disperse the crowd by force. The pacific policy of the sheriff impressed the mob with the idea that the officers were afraid, or at least would do them no harm, and they redoubled their efforts, urged on by a big switchman. At 12 o'clock the door of the prison was broken in with a rail.

As soon as the rapist was brought out of the door calls were heard for a rope; then someone shouted, "Burn him!" But there was no time to make a fire. When Walker got into the lobby a dozen of the men began beating and stabbing him. He was half dragged, half carried to the corner of Front Street and the alley between Sycamore and Mill, and hung to a telegraph pole.

Walker made a desperate resistance. Two men entered his cell first and ordered him to come forth. He refused, and they failing to drag him out, others entered. He scratched and bit his assailants, wounding several of them severely with his teeth. The mob retaliated by striking and cutting him with fists and knives. When he reached the steps leading down to the door he made another stand and was stabbed again and again. By the time he reached the lobby his power to resist was gone, and he was shoved along through the mob of yelling, cursing men and boys, who beat, spat upon and slashed the wretch-like demon. One of the leaders of the mob fell, and the crowd walked ruthlessly over him. He was badly hurt—a jawbone fractured and internal injuries inflicted. After the lynching friends took charge of him.

The mob proceeded north on Front Street with the victim, stopping at Sycamore Street to get a rope from a grocery. "Take him to the iron bridge on Main Street," yelled several men. The men who had hold of the Negro were in a hurry to finish the job, however, and when they reached the telephone pole at the corner of Front Street and the first alley north of Sycamore they stopped. A hastily improvised noose was slipped over the Negro's head, and several young men mounted a pile of lumber near the pole and threw the rope over one of the iron stepping pins. The Negro was lifted up until his feet were three feet above the ground, the rope was made taut, and a corpse dangled in midair. A big fellow who helped lead the mob pulled the Negro's legs until his neck cracked. The wretch's clothes had been torn off, and, as he swung, the man who pulled his legs mutilated the corpse.

One or two knife cuts, more or less, made little difference in the appearance of the dead rapist, however, for before the rope was around his neck his skin was cut almost to ribbons. One pistol shot was fired while the corpse was hanging. A dozen voices protested against the use of firearms, and there was no more shooting. The body was permitted to hang for half an hour, then it was cut down and the rope divided among those who lingered around the scene of the tragedy. Then it was suggested that the corpse be burned, and it was done. The entire performance, from the assault on the jail to the burning of the dead Negro was witnessed by a score or so of policemen and as many deputy sheriffs, but not a hand was lifted to stop the proceedings after the jail door yielded.

As the body hung to the telegraph pole, blood streaming down from the knife wounds in his neck, his hips and lower part of his legs also slashed with knives, the crowd hurled expletives at him, swung the body so that it was dashed against the pole, and, so far from the ghastly sight proving trying to the nerves, the crowd looked on with complaisance, if not with real pleasure. The Negro died hard. The neck was not broken, as the body was drawn up without being given a fall, and death came by strangulation. For fully ten minutes after he was strung up the chest heaved occasionally, and there were convulsive movements of the limbs. Finally he was pronounced dead, and a few minutes later Detective Richardson climbed on a pile of staves and cut the rope. The body fell in a ghastly heap, and the crowd laughed at the sound and crowded around the prostrate body, a few kicking the inanimate carcass.

Detective Richardson, who is also a deputy coroner, then proceeded to impanel the following jury of inquest: J.S. Moody, A.C. Waldran, B.J. Childs, J.N. House, Nelson Bills, T.L. Smith, and A. Newhouse. After viewing the body the inquest was adjourned without any testimony being taken until 9 o'clock this morning. The jury will meet at the coroner's office, 51 Beale Street, upstairs, and decide on a verdict. If no witnesses are forthcoming, the jury will be able to arrive at a verdict just the same, as all members of it saw the lynching. Then someone raised the cry of "Burn him!" It was quickly taken up and soon resounded from a hundred throats. Detective Richardson, for a long time, single-handed, stood the crowd off. He talked and begged the men not to bring disgrace on the city by burning the body, arguing that all the vengeance possible had been wrought.

While this was going on a small crowd was busy starting a fire in the middle of the street. The material was handy. Some bundles of staves were taken from the adjoining lumber yard for kindling. Heavier wood was obtained from the same source, and coal oil from a neighboring grocery. Then the cries of "Burn him! Burn him!" were redoubled.

Half a dozen men seized the naked body. The crowd cheered. They marched to the fire, and giving the body a swing, it was landed in the middle of the fire. There was a cry for more wood, as the fire had begun to die owing to the long delay. Willing hands procured the wood, and it was piled up on the Negro, almost, for a time, obscuring him from view. The head was in plain view, as also were the limbs, and one arm which stood out high above the body, the elbow crooked, held in that position by a stick of wood. In a few moments the hands began to swell, then came great blisters over all the exposed parts of the body; then in places the flesh was burned away and the bones began to show through. It was a horrible sight, one which, perhaps, none there had ever witnessed before. It proved too much for a large part of the crowd and the majority of the mob left very shortly after the burning began.

But a large number stayed, and were not a bit set back by the sight of a human body being burned to ashes. Two or three white women, accompanied by their escorts, pushed to the front to obtain an unobstructed view, and looked on with astonishing coolness and nonchalance. One man and woman brought a little girl, not over twelve years old, apparently their daughter, to view a scene which was calculated to drive sleep from the child's eyes for many nights, if not to produce a permanent injury to her nervous system. The comments of the crowd were varied. Some remarked on the efficacy of this style of cure for rapists, others rejoiced that men's wives and daughters were now safe from this wretch. Some laughed as the flesh cracked and blistered, and while a large number pronounced the burning of a dead body as a useless episode, not in all that throng was a word of sympathy heard for the wretch himself.

The rope that was used to hang the Negro, and also that which was used to lead him from the jail, were eagerly sought by relic hunters. They almost fought for a chance to cut off a piece of rope, and in an incredibly short time both ropes had disappeared and were scattered in the pockets of the crowd in sections of from an inch to six inches long. Others of the relic hunters remained until the ashes cooled to obtain such ghastly relics as the teeth, nails, and bits of charred skin of the immolated victim of his own lust. After burning the body the mob tied a rope around the charred trunk and dragged it down Main Street to the courthouse, where it was hanged to a center pole. The rope broke and the corpse dropped with a thud, but it was again hoisted, the charred legs barely touching the ground. The teeth were knocked out and the fingernails cut off as souvenirs. The crowd made so much noise that the police interfered. Undertaker Walsh was telephoned for, who took charge of the body and carried it to his establishment, where it will be prepared for burial in the potter's field today.

A prelude to this exhibition of nineteenth-century barbarism was the following telegram received by the *Chicago Inter Ocean*, at 2 o'clock, Saturday afternoon—ten hours before the lynching:

MEMPHIS TENN., July 22, To *Inter-Ocean*, Chicago.

Lee Walker, colored man, accused of raping white women, in jail here, will be taken out and burned by whites tonight. Can you send Miss Ida Wells to write it up? Answer. R.M. Martin, with *Public Ledger*.

The *Public Ledger* is one of the oldest evening daily papers in Memphis, and this telegram shows that the intentions of the mob were well known long before they were executed. The personnel of the mob is given by the *Memphis Appeal-Avalanche*. It says, "At first it seemed as if a crowd of roughs were the principals, but as it increased in size, men in all walks of life figured as leaders, although the majority were young men."

This was the punishment meted out to a Negro, charged, not with rape, but attempted assault, and without any proof as to his guilt, for the women were not given a chance to identify him. It was only a little less horrible than the burning alive of Henry Smith, at Paris, Texas, February 1, 1893, or that of Edward Coy, in Texarkana, Texas, February 20, 1892. Both were charged with assault on white women, and both were tied to the stake and burned while yet alive, in the presence of ten thousand persons. In the case of Coy, the white woman in the case applied the match, even while the victim protested his innocence.

The cut which is here given is the exact reproduction of the photograph taken at the scene of the lynching at Clanton, Alabama, August, 1891. The cause for which the man was hanged is given in the words of the mob which were written on the back of the photograph, and they are also given. This photograph was sent to Judge A.W. Tourgee, of Mayville, N.Y.

In some of these cases the mob affects to believe in the Negro's guilt. The world is told that the white woman in the case identifies him, or the prisoner "confesses." But in the lynching which took place in Barnwell County, South Carolina, April 24, 1893, the mob's victim, John Peterson, escaped and placed himself under Governor Tillman's protection; not only did he declare his innocence, but offered to prove an alibi, by white witnesses. Before his witnesses could be brought, the mob arrived at the Governor's mansion and demanded the prisoner. He was given up, and although the white woman in the case said he was not the man, he was hanged twenty-four hours after, and over a thousand bullets fired into his body, on the declaration that "a crime had been committed and someone had to hang for it."

6

HISTORY OF SOME CASES OF RAPE

It has been claimed that the Southern white women have been slandered because, in defending the Negro race from the charge that all colored men, who are lynched, only pay penalty for assaulting women. It is certain that lynching mobs have not only refused to give the Negro a chance to defend himself, but have killed their victim with a full knowledge that the relationship of the alleged assailant with the woman who accused him, was voluntary and clandestine. As a matter of fact, one of the prime causes of the Lynch Law agitation has been a necessity for defending the Negro from this awful charge against him. This defense has been necessary because the apologists for outlawry insist that in no case has the accusing woman been a willing consort of her paramour, who is lynched because overtaken in wrong. It is well known, however, that such is the case. In July of this year, 1894, John Paul Bocock, a Southern white man living in New York, and assistant editor of the *New York Tribune*, took occasion to defy the publication of any instance where the lynched Negro was the victim of a white woman's falsehood. Such cases are not rare, but the press and people conversant with the facts, almost invariably suppress them.

The *New York Sun* of July 30,1894, contained a synopsis of interviews with leading congressmen and editors of the South. Speaker Crisp, of the House of Representatives, who was recently a Judge of the Supreme Court of Georgia, led in declaring that lynching seldom or never took place, save for vile crime against women and children. Dr. Hass, editor of the leading organ of the Methodist Church South, published in its columns that it was his belief that more than three hundred women had been assaulted by Negro men within three months. When asked to prove his charges, or give a single case upon which his "belief" was founded, he said that he could do so, but the details were unfit for publication. No other evidence but his "belief" could be adduced to substantiate this grave charge, yet Bishop Haygood, in the *Forum* of October, 1893, quotes this "belief" in apology for lynching, and voluntarily adds: "It is my opinion that this is an underestimate." The "opinion" of this man, based upon a "belief," had greater weight coming from a man who has posed as a friend to "Our Brother in Black," and was accepted as authority. An interview of Miss Frances E. Willard, the great apostle of temperance, the daughter of abolitionists and a personal friend and helper of many individual colored people, has been quoted in support of the utterance of this calumny against a weak and defenseless race. In the *New York Voice* of October 23, 1890, after a tour in the South, where she was told all these things by the "best white people," she said: "The grogshop is the Negro's center of power. Better whisky and more of it is the rallying cry of great, dark-faced mobs. The colored race multiplies like the locusts of Egypt. The grogshop is its center of power. The safety of woman, of childhood, the home, is menaced in a thousand localities at this moment, so that men dare not go beyond the sight of their own roof-tree."

These charges so often reiterated, have had the effect of fastening the odium upon the race of a peculiar propensity for this foul crime. The Negro is thus forced to a defense of his good name, and this chapter will be devoted to the history of some of the cases where assault upon white women by Negroes is charged. He is not the aggressor in this fight, but the situation demands that the facts be given, and they will speak for themselves. Of the 1,115 Negro men, women and children hanged, shot and roasted alive from January 1, 1882, to January 1, 1894, inclusive, only 348 of that number were charged with rape. Nearly 700 of these persons were lynched for any other reason which could be manufactured by a mob wishing to indulge in a lynching bee.

A WHITE WOMAN'S FALSEHOOD

The *Cleveland, Ohio, Gazette*, January 16, 1892, gives an account of one of these cases of "rape."

Mrs. J.C. Underwood, the wife of a minister of Elyria, Ohio, accused an Afro-American of rape. She told her husband that during his absence in 1888, stumping the state for the Prohibition Party, the man came to the kitchen door, forced his way in the house and insulted her. She tried to drive him out with a heavy poker, but he overpowered and chloroformed her, and when she revived her clothing was torn and she was in a horrible condition. She did not know the man, but could identify him. She subsequently pointed out William Offett, a married man, who was arrested, and, being in Ohio, was granted a trial.

The prisoner vehemently denied the charge of rape, but confessed he went to Mrs. Underwood's residence at her invitation and was criminally intimate with her at her request. This availed him nothing against the sworn testimony of a minister's wife, a lady of the highest respectability. He was found guilty, and entered the penitentiary, December 14, 1888, for fifteen years. Sometime afterwards the woman's remorse led her to confess to her husband that the man was innocent. These are her words: "I met Offett at the postoffice. It was raining. He was polite to me, and as I had several bundles in my arms he offered to carry them home for me, which he did. He had a strange fascination for me, and I invited him to call on me. He called, bringing chestnuts and candy for the children. By this means we got them to leave us alone in the room. Then I sat on his lap. He made a proposal to me and I readily consented. Why I did so I do not know, but that I did is true. He visited me several times after that and each time I was indiscreet. I did not care after the first time. In fact I could not have resisted, and had no desire to resist."

When asked by her husband why she told him she had been outraged, she said: "I had several reasons for telling you. One was the neighbors saw the fellow here, another was, I was afraid I had contracted a loathsome disease, and still another was that I feared I might give birth to a Negro baby. I hoped to save my reputation by telling you a deliberate lie." Her husband, horrified by the confession, had Offett, who had already served four years, released and secured a divorce.

There have been many such cases throughout the South, with the difference that the Southern white men in insensate fury wreak their vengeance without intervention of law upon the Negro who consorts with their women.

TRIED TO MANUFACTURE AN OUTRAGE

The *Memphis (Tenn.) Ledger*, of June 8, 1892, has the following:

If Lillie Bailey, a rather pretty white girl, seventeen years of age,
who is now at the city hospital, would be somewhat less reserved about
her disgrace there would be some very nauseating details in the story of
her life. She is the mother of a little coon. The truth might reveal
fearful depravity or the evidence of a rank outrage. She will not
divulge the name of the man who has left such black evidence of her
disgrace, and in fact says it is a matter in which there can be no
interest to the outside world. She came to Memphis nearly three months
ago, and was taken in at the Woman's Refuge in the southern part of the
city. She remained there until a few weeks ago when the child was born.
The ladies in charge of the Refuge were horrified. The girl was at once
sent to the city hospital, where she has been since May 30. She is a
country girl. She came to Memphis from her father's farm, a short
distance from Hernando, Miss. Just when she left there she would not
say. In fact she says she came to Memphis from Arkansas, and says her
home is in that state. She is rather good looking, has blue eyes, a low
forehead and dark red hair. The ladies at the Woman's Refuge do not know
anything about the girl further than what they learned when she was an
inmate of the institution; and she would not tell much. When the child
was born an attempt was made to get the girl to reveal the name of the
Negro who had disgraced her, she obstinately refused and it was
impossible to elicit any information from her on the subject.

Note the wording: "The truth might reveal fearful depravity or rank outrage." If it had been a white child or if Lillie Bailey had told a pitiful story of Negro outrage, it would have been a case of woman's weakness or assault and she could have remained at the Woman's Refuge. But a Negro child and to withhold its father's name and thus prevent the killing of another Negro "rapist" was a case of "fearful depravity." Had she revealed the father's name, he would have been lynched and his taking off charged to an assault upon a white woman.

BURNED ALIVE FOR ADULTERY

In Texarkana, Arkansas, Edward Coy was accused of assaulting a white woman. The press dispatches of February 18, 1892, told in detail how he was tied to a tree, the flesh cut from his body by men and boys, and after coal oil was poured over him, the woman he had assaulted gladly set fire to him, and 15,000 persons saw him burn to death. October 1, the *Chicago Inter Ocean* contained the following account of that horror from the pen of the "Bystander" Judge Albion W. Tourgee—as the result of his investigations:

1. The woman who was paraded as victim of violence was of bad character; her husband was a drunkard and a gambler.

2. She was publicly reported and generally known to have been criminally intimate with Coy for more than a year previous.

3. She was compelled by threats, if not by violence, to make the charge against the victim.

4. When she came to apply the match Coy asked her if she would burn him after they had "been sweethearting" so long.

5. A large majority of the "superior" white men prominent in the affair are the reputed fathers of mulatto children.

> These are not pleasant facts, but they are illustrative of the vital
> phase of the so-called race question, which should properly be
> designated an earnest inquiry as to the best methods by which religion,
> science, law and political power may be employed to excuse injustice,
> barbarity and crime done to a people because of race and color. There
> can be no possible belief that these people were inspired by any
> consuming zeal to vindicate God's law against miscegenationists of the
> most practical sort. The woman was a willing partner in the victim's
> guilt, and being of the "superior" race must naturally have been more
> guilty.

NOT IDENTIFIED BUT LYNCHED

February 11, 1893, there occurred in Shelby County, Tennessee, the fourth Negro lynching within fifteen months. The three first were lynched in the city of Memphis for firing on white men in self-defense. This Negro, Richard Neal, was lynched a few miles from the city limits, and the following is taken from the *Memphis (Tenn.) Scimitar*:

> As the *Scimitar* stated on Saturday the Negro, Richard Neal, who raped
> Mrs. Jack White near Forest Hill, in this county, was lynched by a mob
> of about 200 white citizens of the neighborhood. Sheriff McLendon,
> accompanied by Deputies Perkins, App and Harvey and a *Scimitar*
> reporter, arrived on the scene of the execution about 3:30 in the
> afternoon. The body was suspended from the first limb of a post oak tree
> by a new quarter-inch grass rope. A hangman's knot, evidently tied by an
> expert, fitted snugly under the left ear of the corpse, and a new hame
> string pinioned the victim's arms behind him. His legs were not tied.
> The body was perfectly limber when the Sheriff's posse cut it down and
> retained enough heat to warm the feet of Deputy Perkins, whose road cart
> was converted into a hearse. On arriving with the body at Forest Hill

the Sheriff made a bargain with a stalwart young man with a blonde mustache and deep blue eyes, who told the *Scimitar* reporter that he was the leader of the mob, to haul the body to Germantown for $3.

When within half-a-mile of Germantown the Sheriff and posse were overtaken by Squire McDonald of Collierville, who had come down to hold the inquest. The Squire had his jury with him, and it was agreed for the convenience of all parties that he should proceed with the corpse to Germantown and conduct the inquiry as to the cause of death. He did so, and a verdict of death from hanging by parties unknown was returned in due form.

The execution of Neal was done deliberately and by the best people of the Collierville, Germantown and Forest Hill neighborhoods, without passion or exhibition of anger.

He was arrested on Friday about ten o'clock, by Constable Bob Cash, who carried him before Mrs. White. She said: "I think he is the man. I am almost certain of it. If he isn't the man he is exactly like him."

The Negro's coat was torn also, and there were other circumstances against him. The committee returned and made its report, and the chairman put the question of guilt or innocence to a vote.

All who thought the proof strong enough to warrant execution were invited to cross over to the other side of the road. Everybody but four or five negroes crossed over.

The committee then placed Neal on a mule with his arms tied behind him, and proceeded to the scene of the crime, followed by the mob. The rope, with a noose already prepared, was tied to the limb nearest the spot where the unpardonable sin was committed, and the doomed man's mule was brought to a standstill beneath it.

Then Neal confessed. He said he was the right man, but denied that he used force or threats to accomplish his purpose. It was a matter of purchase, he claimed, and said the price paid was twenty-five cents. He warned the colored men present to beware of white women and resist temptation, for to yield to their blandishments or to the passions of men, meant death.

While he was speaking, Mrs. White came from her home and calling Constable Cash to one side, asked if he could not save the Negro's life. The reply was, "No," and Mrs. White returned to the house.

When all was in readiness, the husband of Neal's victim leaped upon the mule's back and adjusted the rope around the Negro's neck. No cap was used, and Neal showed no fear, nor did he beg for mercy. The mule was struck with a whip and bounded out from under Neal, leaving him suspended in the air with his feet about three feet from the ground.

DELIVERED TO THE MOB BY THE GOVERNOR OF THE STATE

John Peterson, near Denmark, S.C., was suspected of rape, but escaped, went to Columbia, and placed himself under Gov. Tillman's protection, declaring he too could prove an alibi by white witnesses. A white reporter hearing his declaration volunteered to find these witnesses, and telegraphed the governor that he would be in Columbia with them on Monday. In the meantime the mob at Denmark, learning Peterson's whereabouts, went to the governor and demanded the prisoner. Gov. Tillman, who had during his canvass for reelection the year before, declared that he would lead a mob to lynch a Negro that assaulted a white woman, gave Peterson up to the mob. He was taken back to Denmark, and the white girl in the case as positively declared that he was not the man. But the verdict of the mob was that "the crime had been committed and somebody had to hang for it, and if he, Peterson, was not guilty of that he was of some other crime," and he was hung, and his body riddled with 1,000 bullets.

LYNCHED AS A WARNING

Alabama furnishes a case in point. A colored man named Daniel Edwards, lived near Selma, Alabama, and worked for a family of a farmer near that place. This resulted in an intimacy between the young man and a daughter of the householder, which finally developed in the disgrace of the girl. After the birth of the child, the mother disclosed the fact that Edwards was its father. The relationship had been sustained for more than a year, and yet this colored man was apprehended, thrown into jail from whence he was taken by a mob of one hundred neighbors and hung to a tree and his body riddled with bullets. A dispatch which describes the lynching, ends as follows. "Upon his back was found pinned this morning the following: 'Warning to all Negroes that are too intimate with white girls. This the work of one hundred best citizens of the South Side.'"

There can be no doubt from the announcement made by this "one hundred best citizens" that they understood full well the character of the relationship which existed between Edwards and the girl, but when the dispatches were sent out, describing the affair, it was claimed that Edwards was lynched for rape.

SUPPRESSING THE TRUTH

In a county in Mississippi during the month of July the Associated Press dispatches sent out a report that the sheriff's eight-year-old daughter had been assaulted by a big, black, burly brute who had been promptly lynched. The facts which have since been investigated show that the girl was more than eighteen years old and that she was discovered by her father in this young man's room who was a servant on the place. But these facts the Associated Press has not given to the world, nor did the same agency acquaint the world with the fact that a Negro youth who was lynched in Tuscumbia, Ala., the same year on the same charge told the white girl who accused him before the mob, that he had met her in the woods often by appointment. There is a young mulatto in one of the State prisons of the South today who is there by charge of a young white woman to screen herself. He is a college graduate and had been corresponding with, and clandestinely visiting her until he was surprised and run out of her room en deshabille by her father. He was put in prison in another town to save his life from the mob and his lawyer advised that it were better to save his life by pleading guilty to charges made and being sentenced for years, than to attempt a defense by exhibiting the letters written him by this girl. In the latter event, the mob would surely murder him, while there was a chance for his life by adopting the former course. Names, places and dates are not given for the same reason.

The excuse has come to be so safe, it is not surprising that a Philadelphia girl, beautiful and well educated, and of good family, should make a confession published in all the daily papers of that city October, 1894, that she had been stealing for some time, and that to cover one of her thefts, she had said she had been bound and gagged in her father's house by a colored man, and money stolen therefrom by him. Had this been done in many localities, it would only have been necessary for her to "identify" the first Negro in that vicinity, to have brought about another lynching bee.

A VILE SLANDER WITH SCANT RETRACTION

The following published in the *Cleveland (Ohio) Leader* of Oct. 23, 1894, only emphasizes our demand that a fair trial shall be given those accused of crime, and the protection of the law be extended until time for a defense be granted.

The sensational story sent out last night from Hicksville that a Negro had outraged a little four-year-old girl proves to be a base canard. The correspondents who went into the details should have taken the pains to investigate, and the officials should have known more of the matter before they gave out such grossly exaggerated information.

The Negro, Charles O'Neil, had been working for a couple of women and, it seems, had worked all winter without being remunerated. There is a little girl, and the girl's mother and grandmother evidently started the story with idea of frightening the Negro out of the country and thus balancing accounts. The town was considerably wrought up and for a time things looked serious. The accused had a preliminary hearing today and not an iota of evidence was produced to indicate that such a crime had been committed, or that he had even attempted such an outrage. The

village marshal was frightened nearly out of his wits and did little to
quiet the excitement last night.

The affair was an outrage on the Negro, at the expense of innocent
childhood, a brainless fabrication from start to finish.

The original story was sent throughout this country and England, but the
Cleveland Leader, so far as known, is the only journal which has published these
facts in refutation of the slander so often published against the race. Not only is it
true that many of the alleged cases of rape against the Negro, are like the
foregoing, but the same crime committed by white men against Negro women
and girls, is never punished by mob or the law. A leading journal in South
Carolina openly said some months ago that "it is not the same thing for a white
man to assault a colored woman as for a colored man to assault a white woman,
because the colored woman had no finer feelings nor virtue to be outraged!" Yet
colored women have always had far more reason to complain of white men in this
respect than ever white women have had of Negroes.

ILLINOIS HAS A LYNCHING

In the month of June, 1893, the proud commonwealth of Illinois joined the
ranks of Lynching States. Illinois, which gave to the world the immortal heroes,
Lincoln, Grant and Logan, trailed its banner of justice in the dust—dyed its hands
red in the blood of a man not proven guilty of crime.

June 3,1893, the country about Decatur, one of the largest cities of the state
was startled with the cry that a white woman had been assaulted by a colored
tramp. Three days later a colored man named Samuel Bush was arrested and put
in jail. A white man testified that Bush, on the day of the assault, asked him where
he could get a drink and he pointed to the house where the farmer's wife was
subsequently said to have been assaulted. Bush said he went to the well but did
not go near the house, and did not assault the woman. After he was arrested the
alleged victim did not see him to identify him—he was presumed to be guilty.

The citizens determined to kill him. The mob gathered, went to the jail, met
with no resistance, took the suspected man, dragged him out tearing every stitch
of clothing from his body, then hanged him to a telegraph pole. The grand jury
refused to indict the lynchers though the names of over twenty persons who were
leaders in the mob were well known. In fact twenty-two persons were indicted,
but the grand jurors and the prosecuting attorney disagreed as to the form of the
indictments, which caused the jurors to change their minds. All indictments were
reconsidered and the matter was dropped. Not one of the dozens of men
prominent in that murder have suffered a whit more inconvenience for the
butchery of that man, than they would have suffered for shooting a dog.

COLOR LINE JUSTICE

In Baltimore, Maryland, a gang of white ruffians assaulted a respectable colored girl who was out walking with a young man of her own race. They held her escort and outraged the girl. It was a deed dastardly enough to arouse Southern blood, which gives its horror of rape as excuse for lawlessness, but she was a colored woman. The case went to the courts and they were acquitted.

In Nashville, Tennessee, there was a white man, Pat Hanifan, who outraged a little colored girl, and from the physical injuries received she was ruined for life. He was jailed for six months, discharged, and is now a detective in that city. In the same city, last May, a white man outraged a colored girl in a drug store. He was arrested and released on bail at the trial. It was rumored that five hundred colored men had organized to lynch him. Two hundred and fifty white citizens armed themselves with Winchesters and guarded him. A cannon was placed in front of his home, and the Buchanan Rifles (State Militia) ordered to the scene for his protection. The colored mob did not show up. Only two weeks before, Eph. Grizzard, who had only been charged with rape upon a white woman, had been taken from the jail, with Governor Buchanan and the police and militia standing by, dragged through the streets in broad daylight, knives plunged into him at every step, and with every fiendish cruelty that a frenzied mob could devise, he was at last swung out on the bridge with hands cut to pieces as he tried to climb up the stanchions. A naked, bloody example of the bloodthirstiness of the nineteenth-century civilization of the Athens of the South! No cannon nor military were called out in his defense. He dared to visit a white woman.

At the very moment when these civilized whites were announcing their determination "to protect their wives and daughters," by murdering Grizzard, a white man was in the same jail for raping eight-year-old Maggie Reese, a colored girl. He was not harmed. The "honor" of grown women who were glad enough to be supported by the Grizzard boys and Ed. Coy, as long as the liaison was not known, needed protection; they were white. The outrage upon helpless childhood needed no avenging in this case; she was black.

A white man in Guthrie, Oklahoma Territory, two months after inflicted such injuries upon another colored girl that she died. He was not punished, but an attempt was made in the same town in the month of June to lynch a colored man who visited a white woman.

In Memphis, Tennessee, in the month of June, Ellerton L. Dorr, who is the husband of Russell Hancock's widow, was arrested for attempted rape on Mattie Cole, a neighbor's cook; he was only prevented from accomplishing his purpose by the appearance of Mattie's employer. Dorr's friends say he was drunk and, not responsible for his actions. The grand jury refused to indict him and he was discharged.

In Tallahassee, Florida, a colored girl, Charlotte Gilliam, was assaulted by white men. Her father went to have a warrant for their arrest issued, but the judge refused to issue it.

In Bowling Green, Virginia, Moses Christopher, a colored lad, was charged with assault, September 10. He was indicted, tried, convicted and sentenced to death in one day. In the same state at Danville, two weeks before—August 29,

Thomas J. Penn, a white man, committed a criminal assault upon Lina Hanna, a twelve-year-old colored girl, but he has not been tried, certainly not killed either by the law or the mob.

In Surrey county, Virginia, C.L. Brock, a white man, criminally assaulted a ten-year-old colored girl, and threatened to kill her if she told. Notwithstanding, she confessed to her aunt, Mrs. Alice Bates, and the white brute added further crime by killing Mrs. Bates when she upbraided him about his crime upon her niece. He emptied the contents of his revolver into her body as she lay. Brock has never been apprehended, and no effort has been made to do so by the legal authorities.

But even when punishment is meted out by law to white villians for this horrible crime, it is seldom or never that capital punishment is invoked. Two cases just clipped from the daily papers will suffice to show how this crime is punished when committed by white offenders and black.

LOUISVILLE, KY., October 19.—Smith Young, colored, was today sentenced to be hanged. Young criminally assaulted a six-year-old child about six months ago.

Jacques Blucher, the Pontiac Frenchman who was arrested at that place for a criminal assault on his daughter Fanny on July 29 last, pleaded nolo contendere when placed on trial at East Greenwich, near Providence, R.I., Tuesday, and was sentenced to five years in State Prison.

Charles Wilson was convicted of assault upon seven-year-old Mamie Keys in Philadelphia, in October, and sentenced to ten years in prison. He was white. Indianapolis courts sentenced a white man in September to eight years in prison for assault upon a twelve-year-old white girl.

April 24, 1893, a lynching was set for Denmark, S.C., on the charge of rape. A white girl accused a Negro of assault, and the mob was about to lynch him. A few hours before the lynching three reputable white men rode into the town and solemnly testified that the accused Negro was at work with them 25 miles away on the day and at the hour the crime had been committed. He was accordingly set free. A white person's word is taken as absolutely for as against a Negro.

7

THE CRUSADE JUSTIFIED

(Appeal from America to the World)

It has been urged in criticism of the movement appealing to the English people for sympathy and support in our crusade against Lynch Law that our action was unpatriotic, vindictive and useless. It is not a part of the plan of this pamphlet to make any defense for that crusade nor to indict any apology for the motives which led to the presentation of the facts of American lynchings to the world at large. To those who are not willfully blind and unjustly critical, the record of more than a thousand lynchings in ten years is enough to justify any peaceable movement tending to ameliorate the conditions which led to this unprecedented slaughter of human beings.

If America would not hear the cry of men, women and children whose dying groans ascended to heaven praying for relief, not only for them but for others who might soon be treated as they, then certainly no fair-minded person can charge disloyalty to those who make an appeal to the civilization of the world for such sympathy and help as it is possible to extend. If stating the facts of these lynchings, as they appeared from time to time in the white newspapers of America—the news gathered by white correspondents, compiled by white press bureaus and disseminated among white people—shows any vindictiveness, then the mind which so charges is not amenable to argument.

But it is the desire of this pamphlet to urge that the crusade started and thus far continued has not been useless, but has been blessed with the most salutary results. The many evidences of the good results can not here be mentioned, but the thoughtful student of the situation can himself find ample proof. There need not here be mentioned the fact that for the first time since lynching began, has there been any occasion for the governors of the several states to speak out in reference to these crimes against law and order.

No matter how heinous the act of the lynchers may have been, it was discussed only for a day or so and then dismissed from the attention of the public. In one or two instances the governor has called attention to the crime, but the civil processes entirely failed to bring the murderers to justice. Since the crusade against lynching was started, however, governors of states, newspapers, senators and representatives and bishops of churches have all been compelled to take cognizance of the prevalence of this crime and to speak in one way or another in the defense of the charge against this barbarism in the United States. This has not been because there was any latent spirit of justice voluntarily asserting itself, especially in those who do the lynching, but because the entire American people now feel, both North and South, that they are objects in the gaze of the civilized world and that for every lynching humanity asks that America render its account to civilization and itself.

AWFUL BARBARISM IGNORED

Much has been said during the months of September and October of 1894 about the lynching of six colored men who on suspicion of incendiarism were made the victims of a most barbarous massacre.

They were arrested, one by one, by officers of the law; they were handcuffed and chained together and by the officers of the law loaded in a wagon and deliberately driven into an ambush where a mob of lynchers awaited them. At the time and upon the chosen spot, in the darkness of the night and far removed from the habitation of any human soul, the wagon was halted and the mob fired upon the six manacled men, shooting them to death as no humane person would have shot dogs. Chained together as they were, in their awful struggles after the first volley, the victims tumbled out of the wagon upon the ground and there in the mud, struggling in their death throes, the victims were made the target of the murderous shotguns, which fired into the writhing, struggling, dying mass of humanity, until every spark of life was gone. Then the officers of the law who had them in charge, drove away to give the alarm and to tell the world that they had been waylaid and their prisoners forcibly taken from them and killed.

It has been claimed that the prompt, vigorous and highly commendable steps of the governor of the State of Tennessee and the judge having jurisdiction over the crime, and of the citizens of Memphis generally, was the natural revolt of the humane conscience in that section of the country, and the determination of honest and honorable men to rid the community of such men as those who were guilty of this terrible massacre. It has further been claimed that this vigorous uprising of the people and this most commendably prompt action of the civil authorities, is ample proof that the American people will not tolerate the lynching of innocent men, and that in cases where brutal lynchings have not been promptly dealt with, the crimes on the part of the victims were such as to put them outside the pale of humanity and that the world considered their death a necessary sacrifice for the good of all.

But this line of argument can in no possible way be truthfully sustained. The lynching of the six men in 1894, barbarous as it was, was in no way more barbarous than took nothing more than a passing notice. It was only the other lynchings which preceded it, and of which the public fact that the attention of the civilized world has been called to lynching in America which made the people of Tennessee feel the absolute necessity for a prompt, vigorous and just arraignment of all the murderers connected with that crime. Lynching is no longer "Our Problem," it is the problem of the civilized world, and Tennessee could not afford to refuse the legal measures which Christianity demands shall be used for the punishment of crime.

MEMPHIS THEN AND NOW

Only two years prior to the massacre of the six men near Memphis, that same city took part in a massacre in every way as bloody and brutal as that of September last. It was the murder of three young colored men and who were known to be among the most honorable, reliable, worthy and peaceable colored citizens of the community. All of them were engaged in the mercantile business, being members of a corporation which conducted a large grocery store, and one of the three being a letter carrier in the employ of the government. These three men were arrested for resisting an attack of a mob upon their store, in which melee none of the assailants, who had armed themselves for their devilish deeds by securing court processes, were killed or even seriously injured. But these three men were put in jail, and on three or four nights after their incarceration a mob of less than a dozen men, by collusion with the civil authorities, entered the jail, took the three men from the custody of the law and shot them to death. Memphis knew of this awful crime, knew then and knows today who the men were who committed it, and yet not the first step was ever taken to apprehend the guilty wretches who walk the streets today with the brand of murder upon their foreheads, but as safe from harm as the most upright citizen of that community. Memphis would have been just as calm and complacent and self-satisfied over the murder of the six colored men in 1894 as it was over these three colored men in 1892, had it not recognized the fact that to escape the brand of barbarism it had not only to speak its denunciation but to act vigorously in vindication of its name.

AN ALABAMA HORROR IGNORED

A further instance of this absolute disregard of every principle of justice and the indifference to the barbarism of Lynch Law may be cited here, and is furnished by white residents in the city of Carrolton, Alabama. Several cases of arson had been discovered, and in their search for the guilty parties, suspicion was found to rest upon three men and a woman. The four suspects were Paul Hill, Paul Archer, William Archer, his brother, and a woman named Emma Fair. The prisoners were apprehended, earnestly asserted their innocence, but went to jail without making any resistance. They claimed that they could easily prove their innocence upon trial.

One would suspect that the civilization which defends itself against the barbarisms of Lynch Law by stating that it lynches human beings only when they are guilty of awful attacks upon women and children, would have been very careful to have given these four prisoners, who were simply charged with arson, a fair trial, to which they were entitled upon every principle of law and humanity. Especially would this seem to be the case when if is considered that one of the prisoners charged was a woman, and if the nineteenth century has shown any advancement upon any lines of human action, it is preeminently shown in its reverence, respect and protection of its womanhood. But the people of Alabama failed to have any regard for womanhood whatever.

The three men and the woman were put in jail to await trial. A few days later it was rumored that they were to be subjects of Lynch Law, and, sure enough, at night a mob of lynchers went to the jail, not to avenge any awful crime against womanhood, but to kill four people who had been suspected of setting a house on fire. They were caged in their cells, helpless and defenseless; they were at the mercy of civilized white Americans, who, armed with shotguns, were there to maintain the majesty of American law. And most effectively was their duty done by these splendid representatives of Governor Fishback's brave and honorable white southerners, who resent "outside interference." They lined themselves up in the most effective manner and poured volley after volley into the bodies of their helpless, pleading victims, who in their bolted prison cells could do nothing but suffer and die. Then these lynchers went quietly away and the bodies of the woman and three men were taken out and buried with as little ceremony as men would bury hogs.

No one will say that the massacre near Memphis in 1894 was any worse than this bloody crime of Alabama in 1892. The details of this shocking affair were given to the public by the press, but public sentiment was not moved to action in the least; it was only a matter of a day's notice and then went to swell the list of murders which stand charged against the noble, Christian people of Alabama.

AMERICA AWAKENED

But there is now an awakened conscience throughout the land, and Lynch Law can not flourish in the future as it has in the past. The close of the year 1894 witnessed an aroused interest, an assertative humane principle which must tend to the extirpation of that crime. The awful butchery last mentioned failed to excite more than a passing comment In 1894, but far different is it today. Gov. Jones, of Alabama, in 1893 dared to speak out against the rule of the mob in no uncertain terms. His address indicated a most helpful result of the present agitation. In face of the many denials of the outrages on the one hand and apologies for lynchers on the other, Gov. Jones admits the awful lawlessness charged and refuses to join in the infamous plea made to condone the crime. No stronger nor more effective words have been said than those following from Gov. Jones.

While the ability of the state to deal with open revolts against the supremacy of its laws has been ably demonstrated, I regret that deplorable acts of violence have been perpetrated, in at least four instances, within the past two years by mobs, whose sudden work and quick dispersions rendered it impossible to protect their victims. Within the past two years nine prisoners, who were either in jail or in the custody of the officers, have been taken from them without resistance, and put to death. There was doubt of the guilt of the defendants in most of these cases, and few of them were charged with capital offenses. None of them involved the crime of rape. The largest rewards allowed by law were offered for the apprehension of the offenders, and officers were charged to a vigilant performance of their duties, and aided in some instances by the services of skilled detectives; but not a single arrest has been made and the grand juries in these counties have returned no bills of indictment. This would indicate either that local public sentiment approved these acts of violence or was too weak to punish them, or that the officers charged with that duty were in some way lacking in their performance. The evil cannot be cured or remedied by silence as to its existence. Unchecked, it will continue until it becomes a reproach to our good name, and a menace to our prosperity and peace; and it behooves you to exhaust all remedies within your power to find better preventives for such crimes.

A FRIENDLY WARNING

From England comes a friendly voice which must give to every patriotic citizen food for earnese thought. Writing from London, to the *Chicago Inter Ocean*, Nov. 25, 1894, the distinguished compiler of our last census, Hon. Robert P. Porter, gives the American people a most interesting review of the antilynching crusade in England, submitting editorial opinions from all sections of England and Scotland, showing the consensus of British opinion on this subject. It hardly need be said, that without exception, the current of English thought deprecates the rule of mob law, and the conscience of England is shocked by the revelation made during the present crusade. In his letter Mr. Porter says:

While some English journals have joined certain American journals in ridiculing the well-meaning people who have formed the antilynching committee, there is a deep under current on this subject which is injuring the Southern States far more than those who have not been drawn into the question of English investment for the South as I have can surmise. This feeling is by no means all sentiment. An Englishman whose word and active cooperation could send a million sterling to any legitimate Southern enterprise said the other day: "I will not invest a farthing in States where these horrors occur. I have no particular sympathy with the antilynching committee, but such outrages indicate to my mind that where life is held to be of such little value there is even less assurance that the laws will protect property. As I understand it the States, not the national government, control in such matters, and where those laws are strongest there is the best field for British capital."

Probably the most bitter attack on the antilynching committee has come from the *London Times*. Those Southern Governors who had their bombastic letters published in the *Times*, with favorable editorial comment, may have had their laugh at the antilynchers here too soon. A few days ago, in commenting on an interesting communication from Richard H. Edmonds, editor of the *Manufacturer's Record*, setting forth the industrial advantages of the Southern States, which was published in its columns, the *Times* says:

Without in any way countenancing the impertinence of "antilynching" committee, we may say that a state of things in which the killing of

Negroes by bloodthirsty mobs is an incident of not unfrequent occurrence is not conducive to success in industry. Its existence, however, is a serious obstacle to the success of the South in industry; for even now Negro labor, which means at best inefficient labor, must be largely relied on there, and its efficiency must be still further diminished by spasmodic terrorism.

Those interested in the development of the resources of the Southern States, and no one in proportion to his means has shown more faith in the progress of the South than the writer of this article, must take hold of this matter earnestly and intelligently. Sneering at the antilynching committee will do no good. Back of them, in fact, if not in form, is the public opinion of Great Britain. Even the *Times* cannot deny this. It may not be generally known in the United States, but while the Southern and some of the Northern newspapers are making a target of Miss Wells, the young colored woman who started this English movement, and cracking their jokes at the expense of Miss Florence Balgarnie, who, as honorable secretary, conducts the committee's correspondence, the strongest sort of sentiment is really at the back of the movement. Here we have crystallized every phase of political opinion. Extreme Unionists like the Duke of Argyll and advanced home rulers such as Justin McCarthy; Thomas Burt, the labor leader; Herbert Burrows, the Socialist, and Tom Mann, representing all phases of the Labor party, are cooperating with conservatives like Sir T. Eldon Gorst. But the real strength of this committee is not visible to the casual observer. As a matter of fact it represents many of the leading and most powerful British journals. A.E. Fletcher is editor of the *London Daily Chronicle*; P.W. Clayden is prominent in the counsels of the *London Daily News*; Professor James Stuart is Gladstone's great friend and editor of the *London Star*, William Byles is editor and proprietor of the *Bradford Observer*, Sir Hugh Gilzen Reid is a leading Birmingham editor; in short, this committee has secured if not the leading editors, certainly important and warm friends, representing the Manchester Guardian, the *Leeds Mercury*, the *Plymouth Western News, Newcastle Leader*, the *London Daily Graphic*, the *Westminster Gazette*, the *London Echo*, a host of minor papers all over the kingdom, and practically the entire religious press of the kingdom.

The greatest victory for the antilynchers comes this morning in the publication in the *London Times* of William Lloyd Garrison's letter. This letter will have immense effect here. It may have been printed in full in the United States, but nevertheless I will quote a paragraph which will strengthen the antilynchers greatly in their crusade here:

A year ago the South derided and resented Northern protests; today it listens, explains and apologizes for its uncovered cruelties. Surely a great triumph for a little woman to accomplish! It is the power of truth simply and unreservedly spoken, for her language was inadequate to describe the horrors exposed.

If the Southern states are wise, and I say this with the earnestness of a friend and one who has built a home in the mountain regions of the South and thrown his lot in with them, they will not only listen, but stop lawlessness of all kinds. If they do, and thus secure the confidence of Englishmen, we may in the next decade realize some of the hopes for the new South we have so fondly cherished.

8

MISS WILLARD'S ATTITUDE

No class of American citizens stands in greater need of the humane and thoughtful consideration of all sections of our country than do the colored people, nor does any class exceed us in the measure of grateful regard for acts of kindly interest in our behalf. It is, therefore, to us, a matter of keen regret that a Christian organization, so large and influential as the Woman's Christian Temperance Union, should refuse to give its sympathy and support to our oppressed people who ask no further favor than the promotion of public sentiment which shall guarantee to every person accused of crime the safeguard of a fair and impartial trial, and protection from butchery by brutal mobs. Accustomed as we are to the indifference and apathy of Christian people, we would bear this instance of ill fortune in silence, had not Miss Willard gone out of her way to antagonize the cause so dear to our hearts by including in her Annual Address to the W.C.T.U. Convention at Cleveland, November 5, 1894, a studied, unjust and wholly unwarranted attack upon our work.

In her address Miss Willard said:

The zeal for her race of Miss Ida B. Wells, a bright young colored woman, has, it seems to me, clouded her perception as to who were her friends and well-wishers in all high-minded and legitimate efforts to banish the abomination of lynching and torture from the land of the free and the home of the brave. It is my firm belief that in the statements made by Miss Wells concerning white women having taken the initiative in nameless acts between the races she has put an imputation upon half the white race in this country that is unjust, and, save in the rarest exceptional instances, wholly without foundation. This is the unanimous opinion of the most disinterested and observant leaders of opinion whom I have consulted on the subject, and I do not fear to say that the laudable efforts she is making are greatly handicapped by statements of this kind, nor to urge her as a friend and well-wisher to banish from her vocabulary all such allusions as a source of weakness to the cause she has at heart.

This paragraph, brief as it is, contains two statements which have not the slightest foundation in fact. At no time, nor in any place, have I made statements "concerning white women having taken the initiative in nameless acts between the races." Further, at no time, or place nor under any circumstance, have I directly or inferentially "put an imputation upon half the white race in this country" and I challenge this "friend and well-wisher" to give proof of the truth of her charge. Miss Willard protests against lynching in one paragraph and then, in the next, deliberately misrepresents my position in order that she may criticise a movement, whose only purpose is to protect our oppressed race from vindictive slander and Lynch Law.

What I have said and what I now repeat—in answer to her first charge—is, that colored men have been lynched for assault upon women, when the facts were plain that the relationship between the victim lynched and the alleged victim of his assault was voluntary, clandestine and illicit. For that very reason we maintain, that, in every section of our land, the accused should have a fair, impartial trial, so that a man who is colored shall not be hanged for an offense, which, if he were white, would not be adjudged a crime. Facts cited in another chapter—"History of Some Cases of Rape"—amply maintain this position. The publication of these facts in defense of the good name of the race casts no "imputation upon half the white race in this country" and no such imputation can be inferred except by persons deliberately determined to be unjust.

But this is not the only injury which this cause has suffered at the hands of our "friend and well-wisher." It has been said that the Women's Christian Temperance Union, the most powerful organization of women in America, was misrepresented by me while I was in England. Miss Willard was in England at the time and knowing that no such misrepresentation came to her notice, she has permitted that impression to become fixed and widespread, when a word from her would have made the facts plain.

I never at any time or place or in any way misrepresented that organization. When asked what concerted action had been taken by churches and great moral agencies in America to put down Lynch Law, I was compelled in truth to say that no such action had occurred, that pulpit, press and moral agencies in the main were silent and for reasons known to themselves, ignored the awful conditions which to the English people appeared so abhorent. Then the question was asked what the great moral reformers like Miss Frances Willard and Mr. Moody had done to suppress Lynch Law and again I answered nothing. That Mr. Moody had never said a word against lynching in any of his trips to the South, or in the North either, so far as was known, and that Miss Willard's only public utterance on the situation had condoned lynching and other unjust practices of the South against the Negro. When proof of these statements was demanded, I sent a letter containing a copy of the *New York Voice*, Oct. 23,1890, in which appeared Miss Willard's own words of wholesale slander against the colored race and condonation of Southern white people's outrages against us. My letter in part reads as follows:

But Miss Willard, the great temperance leader, went even further in putting the seal of her approval upon the southerners' method of dealing with the Negro. In October, 1890, the Women's Christian Temperance Union held its national meeting at Atlanta, Georgia. It was the first time in the history of the organization that it had gone south for a national meeting, and met the southerners in their own homes. They were welcomed with open arms. The governor of the state and the legislature gave special audiences in the halls of state legislation to the temperance workers. They set out to capture the northerners to their way of seeing things, and without troubling to hear the Negro side of the question, these temperance people accepted the white man's story of the problem with which he had to deal. State organizers were appointed that year, who had gone through the southern states since then, but in obedience to southern prejudices have confined their work to white persons only. It is only after Negroes are in prison for crimes that efforts of these temperance women are exerted without regard to "race, color, or previous condition." No "ounce of prevention" is used in their case; they are black, and if these women went among the Negroes for this work, the whites would not receive them. Except here and there, are found no temperance workers of the Negro race; "the great dark-faced mobs" are left the easy prey of the saloonkeepers.

There was pending in the National Congress at this time a Federal Election Bill, the object being to give the National Government control of the national elections in the several states. Had this bill become a law, the Negro, whose vote has been systematically suppressed since 1875 in the southern states, would have had the protection of the National Government, and his vote counted. The South would have been no longer "solid"; the Southerners saw that the balance of power which they unlawfully held in the House of Representatives and the Electoral College, based on the Negro population, would be wrested from them. So they nick-named the pending elections law the "Force Bill"—probably because it would force them to disgorge their ill-gotten political gains—and defeated it. While it was being discussed, the question was submitted to Miss Willard: "What do you think of the race problem and the Force Bill?"

Said Miss Willard: "Now, as to the 'race problem' in its minified, current meaning, I am a true lover of the southern people—have spoken and worked in, perhaps, 200 of their towns and cities; have been taken into their love and confidence at scores of hospitable firesides; have heard them pour out their hearts in the splendid frankness of their impetuous natures. And I have said to them at such times: 'When I go North there will be wafted to you no word from pen or voice that is not loyal to what we are saying here and now.' Going South, a woman, a temperance woman, and a Northern temperance woman—three great barriers to their good will yonder—I was received by them with a confidence that was one of the most delightful surprises of my life. I think we have wronged the South, though we did not mean to do so. The reason was, in part, that we had irreparably wronged ourselves by putting no safeguards on the ballot box at the North that would sift out alien illiterates. They rule our cities today; the saloon is their palace, and the toddy stick their sceptre. It is not fair that they should vote, nor is it fair that a plantation Negro, who can neither read nor write, whose ideas are bounded by the fence of his own field and the price of his own mule, should be entrusted with the ballot. We ought to have put an educational test upon that ballot from the first. The Anglo-Saxon race will never submit to be dominated by the Negro so long as his altitude reaches no higher than the personal liberty of the saloon, and the power of appreciating the amount of liquor that a dollar will buy. New England would no more submit to this than South Carolina. 'Better whisky and more of it' has been the rallying cry of great dark-faced mobs in the Southern localities where local option was snowed under by the colored vote. Temperance has no enemy like that, for it is unreasoning and unreasonable. Tonight it promises in a great congregation to vote for temperance at the polls tomorrow; but tomorrow twenty-five cents changes that vote in favor of the liquor-seller.

"I pity the southerners, and I believe the great mass of them are as conscientious and kindly intentioned toward the colored man as an equal number of white church-members of the North. Would-be demagogues lead the colored people to destruction. Half-drunken white roughs murder them at the polls, or intimidate them so that they do not vote. But the better class of people must not be blamed for this, and a more thoroughly American population than the Christian people of the South does not exist. They have the traditions, the kindness, the probity, the courage of our forefathers. The problem on their hands is immeasurable. The colored race multiplies like the locusts of Egypt. The grog-shop is its center of power. 'The safety of woman, of childhood, of the home, is menaced in a thousand localities at this moment, so that the men dare not go beyond the sight of their own roof-tree.' How little we know of all this, seated in comfort and affluence here at the North, descanting upon the rights of every man to cast one vote and have it fairly counted; that well-worn shibboleth invoked once more to dodge a living issue.

"The fact is that illiterate colored men will not vote at the South until the white population chooses to have them do so; and under similar conditions they would not at the North." Here we have Miss Willard's words in full, condoning fraud, violence, murder, at the ballot box; rapine, shooting, hanging and burning; for all these things are done and being done now by the Southern white people. She does not stop there, but goes a step further to aid them in blackening the good name of an entire race, as shown by the sentences quoted in the paragraph above. These utterances, for which the colored people have never forgiven Miss Willard, and which Frederick Douglass has denounced as false, are to be found in full in the Voice of October 23,1890, a temperance organ published at New York City.

This letter appeared in the May number of *Fraternity*, the organ of the first Anti-Lynching society of Great Britain. When Lady Henry Somerset learned through Miss Florence Balgarnie that this letter had been published she informed me that if the interview was published she would take steps to let the public know that my statements must be received with caution. As I had no money to pay the printer to suppress the edition which was already published and these ladies did not care to do so, the May number of *Fraternity* was sent to its subscribers as usual. Three days later there appeared in the daily *Westminster Gazette* an "interview" with Miss Willard, written by Lady Henry Somerset, which was so subtly unjust in its wording that I was forced to reply in my own defense. In that reply I made only statements which, like those concerning Miss Willard's *Voice* interview, have not been and cannot be denied. It was as follows:

LADY HENRY SOMERSET'S INTERVIEW WITH MISS WILLARD

To the Editor of the *Westminster Gazette.* Sir—The interview published in your columns today hardly merits a reply, because of the indifference to suffering manifested. Two ladies are represented sitting under a tree at Reigate, and, after some preliminary remarks on the terrible subject of lynching, Miss Willard laughingly replies by cracking a joke. And the concluding sentence of the interview shows the object is not to determine how best they may help the Negro who is being hanged, shot and burned, but "to guard Miss Willard's reputation."

With me it is not myself nor my reputation, but the life of my people, which is at stake, and I affirm that this is the first time to my knowledge that Miss Willard has said a single word in denunciation of lynching or demand for law. The year 1890, the one in which the interview appears, had a larger lynching record than any previous year, and the number and territory have increased, to say nothing of the human beings burnt alive.

If so earnest as she would have the English public believe her to be, why was she silent when five minutes were given me to speak last June at Princes' Hall, and in Holborn Town Hall this May? I should say it was as President of the Women's Christian Temperance Union of America she is timid, because all these unions in the South emphasize the hatred of the Negro by excluding him. There is not a single colored woman admitted to the Southern W.C.T.U., but still Miss Willard blames the Negro for the defeat of Prohibition in the South. Miss Willard quotes from *Fraternity*, but forgets to add my immediate recognition of her presence on the platform at Holborn Town Hall, when, amidst many other resolutions on temperance and other subjects in which she is interested, time was granted to carry an anti-lynching resolution. I was so thankful for this crumb of her speechless presence that I hurried off to the editor of *Fraternity* and added a postscript to my article blazoning forth that fact.

Any statements I have made concerning Miss Willard are confirmed by the Hon. Frederick Douglass (late United States minister to Hayti) in a speech delivered by him in Washington in January of this year, which has since been published in a pamphlet. The fact is, Miss Willard is no better or worse than the great bulk of white Americans on the Negro questions. They are all afraid to speak out, and it is only British public opinion which will move them, as I am thankful to see it has already begun to move Miss Willard. I am, etc.,

May 21

IDA B. WELLS

Unable to deny the truth of these assertions, the charge has been made that I have attacked Miss Willard and misrepresented the W.C.T.U. If to state facts is misrepresentation, then I plead guilty to the charge.

I said then and repeat now, that in all the ten terrible years of shooting, hanging and burning of men, women and children in America, the Women's Christian Temperance Union never suggested one plan or made one move to prevent those awful crimes. If this statement is untrue the records of that organization would disprove it before the ink is dry. It is clearly an issue of fact and in all fairness this charge of misrepresentation should either be substantiated or withdrawn.

It is not necessary, however, to make any representation concerning the W.C.T.U. and the lynching question. The record of that organization speaks for itself. During all the years prior to the agitation begun against Lynch Law, in which years men, women and children were scourged, hanged, shot and burned, the W.C.T.U. had no word, either of pity or protest; its great heart, which concerns itself about humanity the world over, was, toward our cause, pulseless as a stone. Let those who deny this speak by the record. Not until after the first British campaign, in 1893, was even a resolution passed by the body which is the self-constituted guardian for "God, home and native land."

Nor need we go back to other years. The annual session of that organization held in Cleveland in November, 1894, made a record which confirms and emphasizes the silence charged against it. At that session, earnest efforts were made to secure the adoption of a resolution of protest against lynching. At that very time two men were being tried for the murder of six colored men who were arrested on charge of barn burning, chained together, and on pretense of being taken to jail, were driven into the woods where they were ambushed and all six shot to death. The six widows of the butchered men had just finished the most pathetic recital ever heard in any court room, and the mute appeal of twenty-seven orphans for justice touched the stoutest hearts. Only two weeks prior to the session, Gov. Jones of Alabama, in his last message to the retiring state legislature, cited the fact that in the two years just past, nine colored men had been taken from the legal authorities by lynching mobs and butchered in cold blood—and not one of these victims was even charged with an assault upon womanhood.

It was thought that this great organization, in face of these facts, would not hesitate to place itself on record in a resolution of protest against this awful brutality towards colored people. Miss Willard gave assurance that such a resolution would be adopted, and that assurance was relied on. The record of the session shows in what good faith that assurance was kept. After recommending an expression against Lynch Law, the President attacked the antilynching movement, deliberately misrepresenting my position, and in her annual address, charging me with a statement I never made.

Further than that, when the committee on resolutions reported their work, not a word was said against lynching. In the interest of the cause I smothered the resentment. I felt because of the unwarranted and unjust attack of the President, and labored with members to secure an expression of some kind, tending to abate the awful slaughter of my race. A resolution against lynching was introduced by Mrs. Fessenden and read, and then that great Christian body, which in its resolutions had expressed itself in opposition to the social amusement of card playing, athletic sports and promiscuous dancing; had protested against the licensing of saloons, inveighed against tobacco, pledged its allegiance to the Prohibition party, and thanked the Populist party in Kansas, the Republican party in California and the Democratic party in the South, wholly ignored the seven millions of colored people of this country whose plea was for a word of sympathy and support for the movement in their behalf. The resolution was not adopted, and the convention adjourned.

In the *Union Signal* Dec. 6, 1894, among the resolutions is found this one:

Resolved, That the National W.C.T.U, which has for years counted among
its departments that of peace and arbitration, is utterly opposed to all
lawless acts in any and all parts of our common lands and it urges these
principles upon the public, praying that the time may speedily come
when no human being shall be condemned without due process of law; and
when the unspeakable outrages which have so often provoked such
lawlessness shall be banished from the world, and childhood, maidenhood
and womanhood shall no more be the victims of atrocities worse than
death.

This is not the resolution offered by Mrs. Fessenden. She offered the one passed last year by the W.C.T.U. which was a strong unequivocal denunciation of lynching. But she was told by the chairman of the committee on resolutions, Mrs. Rounds, that there was already a lynching resolution in the hands of the committee. Mrs. Fessenden yielded the floor on that assurance, and no resolution of any kind against lynching was submitted and none was voted upon, not even the one above, taken from the columns of the *Union Signal*, the organ of the national W.C.T.U!

Even the wording of this resolution which was printed by the W.C.T.U., reiterates the false and unjust charge which has been so often made as an excuse for lynchers. Statistics show that less than one-third of the lynching victims are hanged, shot and burned alive for "unspeakable outrages against womanhood, maidenhood and childhood;" and that nearly a thousand, including women and children, have been lynched upon any pretext whatsoever; and that all have met death upon the unsupported word of white men and women. Despite these facts this resolution which was printed, cloaks an apology for lawlessness, in the same paragraph which affects to condemn it, where it speaks of "the unspeakable outrages which have so often provoked such lawlessness."

Miss Willard told me the day before the resolutions were offered that the Southern women present had held a caucus that day. This was after I, as fraternal delegate from the Woman's Mite Missionary Society of the A.M.E. Church at Cleveland, O., had been introduced to tender its greetings. In so doing I expressed the hope of the colored women that the W.C.T.U. would place itself on record as opposed to lynching which robbed them of husbands, fathers, brothers and sons and in many cases of women as well. No note was made either in the daily papers or the *Union Signal* of that introduction and greeting, although every other incident of that morning was published. The failure to submit a lynching resolution and the wording of the one above appears to have been the result of that Southern caucus.

On the same day I had a private talk with Miss Willard and told her she had been unjust to me and the cause in her annual address, and asked that she correct the statement that I had misrepresented the W.C.T.U, or that I had "put an imputation on one-half the white race in this country." She said that somebody in England told her it was a pity that I attacked the white women of America. "Oh," said I, "then you went out of your way to prejudice me and my cause in your annual address, not upon what you had heard me say, but what somebody had told you I said?" Her reply was that I must not blame her for her rhetorical expressions—that I had my way of expressing things and she had hers. I told her I most assuredly did blame her when those expressions were calculated to do such harm. I waited for an honest an unequivocal retraction of her statements based on "hearsay." Not a word of retraction or explanation was said in the convention and I remained misrepresented before that body through her connivance and consent.

The editorial notes in the *Union Signal*, Dec. 6, 1894, however, contains the following:

In her repudiation of the charges brought by Miss Ida Wells against white women as having taken the initiative in nameless crimes between the races, Miss Willard said in her annual address that this statement "put an unjust imputation upon half the white race." But as this expression has been misunderstood she desires to declare that she did not intend a literal interpretation to be given to the language used, but employed it to express a tendency that might ensue in public thought as a result of utterances so sweeping as some that have been made by Miss Wells.

Because this explanation is as unjust as the original offense, I am forced in self-defense to submit this account of differences. I desire no quarrel with the W.C.T.U., but my love for the truth is greater than my regard for an alleged friend who, through ignorance or design misrepresents in the most harmful way the cause of a long suffering race, and then unable to maintain the truth of her attack excuses herself as it were by the wave of the hand, declaring that "she did not intend a literal interpretation to be given to the language used." When the lives of men, women and children are at stake, when the inhuman butchers of innocents attempt to justify their barbarism by fastening upon a whole race the obloque of the most infamous of crimes, it is little less than criminal to apologize for the butchers today and tomorrow to repudiate the apology by declaring it a figure of speech.

9

LYNCHING RECORD FOR 1894

The following tables are based on statistics taken from the columns of the *Chicago Tribune*, Jan. 1, 1895. They are a valuable appendix to the foregoing pages. They show, among other things, that in Louisiana, April 23-28, eight Negroes were lynched because one white man was killed by the Negro, the latter acting in self defense. Only seven of them are given in the list.

Near Memphis, Tenn., six Negroes were lynched—this time charged with burning barns. A trial of the indicted resulted in an acquittal, although it was shown on trial that the lynching was prearranged for them. Six widows and twenty-seven orphans are indebted to this mob for their condition, and this lynching swells the number to eleven Negroes lynched in and about Memphis since March 9, 1892.

In Brooks County, Ga., Dec. 23, while this Christian country was preparing for Christmas celebration, seven Negroes were lynched in twenty-four hours because they refused, or were unable to tell the whereabouts of a colored man named Pike, who killed a white man. The wives and daughters of these lynched men were horribly and brutally outraged by the murderers of their husbands and fathers. But the mob has not been punished and again women and children are robbed of their protectors whose blood cries unavenged to Heaven and humanity. Georgia heads the list of lynching states.

MURDER

Jan. 9, Samuel Smith, Greenville, Ala., Jan. 11, Sherman Wagoner, Mitchell, Ind.; Jan. 12, Roscoe Parker, West Union, Ohio; Feb. 7, Henry Bruce, Gulch Co., Ark.; March 5, Sylvester Rhodes, Collins, Ga.; March 15, Richard Puryea, Stroudsburg, Pa.; March 29, Oliver Jackson, Montgomery, Ala.; March 30, ——— Saybrick, Fisher's Ferry, Miss.; April 14, William Lewis, Lanison, Ala.; April 23, Jefferson Luggle, Cherokee, Kan.; April 23, Samuel Slaugate, Tallulah, La.; April 23, Thomas Claxton, Tallulah, La.; April 23, David Hawkins, Tallulah, La.; April 27, Thel Claxton, Tallulah, La.; April 27, Comp Claxton, Tallulah, La.; April 27, Scot Harvey, Tallulah, La.; April 27, Jerry McCly, Tallulah, La.; May 17, Henry Scott, Jefferson, Tex.; May 15, Coat Williams, Pine Grove, Fla.; June 2, Jefferson Crawford, Bethesda, S.C.; June 4, Thondo Underwood, Monroe, La.; June 8, Isaac Kemp, Cape Charles, Va.; June 13, Lon Hall, Sweethouse, Tex.; June 13, Bascom Cook, Sweethouse, Tex.; June 15, Luke Thomas, Biloxi, Miss.; June 29, John Williams, Sulphur, Tex.; June 29, Ulysses Hayden, Monett, Mo.; July 6, ——— Hood, Amite, Miss.; July 7, James Bell, Charlotte, Tenn.; Sept. 2, Henderson Hollander, Elkhorn, W. Va.; Sept. 14, Robert Williams, Concordia Parish, La.; Sept. 22, Luke Washington, Meghee, Ark.; Sept. 22, Richard Washington, Meghee, Ark.; Sept. 22, Henry Crobyson, Meghee, Ark.; Nov. 10, Lawrence Younger, Lloyd, Va.; Dec. 17, unknown Negro, Williamston, S.C.; Dec. 23,

Samuel Taylor, Brooks County, Ga.; Dec. 23, Charles Frazier, Brooks County, Ga.; Dec. 23, Samuel Pike, Brooks County, Ga.; Dec. 22, Harry Sherard, Brooks County, Ga.; Dec. 23, unknown Negro, Brooks County, Ga.; Dec. 23, unknown Negro, Brooks County, Ga.; Dec. 23, unknown Negro, Brooks County, Ga.; Dec. 26, Daniel McDonald, Winston County, Miss.; Dec. 23, William Carter, Winston County, Miss.

RAPE

Jan. 17, John Buckner, Valley Park, Mo.; Jan. 21, M.G. Cambell, Jellico Mines, Ky.; Jan. 27, unknown, Verona, Mo.; Feb. 11, Henry McCreeg, near Pioneer, Tenn.; April 6, Daniel Ahren, Greensboro, Ga.; April 15, Seymour Newland, Rushsylvania, Ohio; April 26, Robert Evarts, Jamaica, Ga.; April 27, James Robinson, Manassas, Va.; April 27, Benjamin White, Manassas, Va.; May 15, Nim Young, Ocala, Fla.; May 22, unknown, Miller County, Ga.; June 13, unknown, Blackshear, Ga.; June 18, Owen Opliltree, Forsyth, Ga.; June 22, Henry Capus, Magnolia, Ark.; June 26, Caleb Godly, Bowling Green, Ky.; June 28, Fayette Franklin, Mitchell, Ga.; July 2, Joseph Johnson, Hiller's Creek, Mo.; July 6, Lewis Bankhead, Cooper, Ala.; July 16, Marion Howard, Scottsville, Ky.; July 20, William Griffith, Woodville, Tex.; Aug. 12, William Nershbread, Rossville, Tenn.; Aug. 14, Marshall Boston, Frankfort, Ky; Sept. 19, David Gooseby, Atlanta, Ga.; Oct. 15, Willis Griffey, Princeton, Ky; Nov. 8, Lee Lawrence, Jasper County, Ga.; Nov. 10, Needham Smith, Tipton County, Tenn.; Nov. 14, Robert Mosely, Dolinite, Ala.; Dec. 4, William Jackson, Ocala, Fla.; Dec. 18, unknown, Marion County, Fla.

UNKNOWN OFFENSES

March 6, Lamsen Gregory, Bell's Depot, Tenn.; March 6, unknown woman, near Marche, Ark.; April 14, Alfred Brenn, Calhoun, Ga.; June 8, Harry Gill, West Lancaster, S.C.; Nov. 23, unknown, Landrum, S.C.; Dec. 5, Mrs. Teddy Arthur, Lincoln County, W. Va.

DESPERADO

Jan. 14, Charles Willis, Ocala, Fla.

SUSPECTED INCENDIARISM

Jan. 18, unknown, Bayou Sarah, La.

SUSPECTED ARSON

June 14, J.H. Dave, Monroe, La.

ENTICING SERVANT AWAY

Feb. 10, —— Collins, Athens, Ga.

TRAIN WRECKING

Feb. 10, Jesse Dillingham, Smokeyville, Tex.

HIGHWAY ROBBERY

June 3, unknown, Dublin, Ga.

INCENDIARISM

Nov. 8, Gabe Nalls, Blackford, Ky.; Nov. 8, Ulysses Nails, Blackford, Ky.

ARSON

Dec. 20, James Allen, Brownsville, Tex.

ASSAULT

Dec. 23, George King, New Orleans, La.

NO OFFENSE

Dec. 28, Scott Sherman, Morehouse Parish, La.

BURGLARY

May 29, Henry Smith, Clinton, Miss.; May 29, William James, Clinton, Miss.

ALLEGED RAPE

June 4, Ready Murdock, Yazoo, Miss.

ATTEMPTED RAPE

July 14, unknown Negro, Biloxi, Miss.; July 26, Vance McClure, New Iberia, La.; July 26, William Tyler, Carlisle, Ky.; Sept. 14, James Smith, Stark, Fla.; Oct. 8, Henry Gibson, Fairfield, Tex.; Oct. 20, —— Williams, Upper Marlboro, Md.; June 9, Lewis Williams, Hewett Springs, Miss.; June 28, George Linton, Brookhaven, Miss.; June 28, Edward White, Hudson, Ala.; July 6, George Pond, Fulton, Miss.; July 7, Augustus Pond, Tupelo, Miss.

72

RACE PREJUDICE

June 10, Mark Jacobs, Bienville, La.; July 24, unknown woman, Sampson County, Miss.

INTRODUCING SMALLPOX

June 10, James Perry, Knoxville, Ark.

KIDNAPPING

March 2, Lentige, Harland County, Ky.

CONSPIRACY

May 29, J.T. Burgis, Palatka, Fla.

HORSE STEALING

June 20, Archie Haynes, Mason County, Ky.; June 20, Burt Haynes, Mason County, Ky.; June 20, William Haynes, Mason County, Ky.

WRITING LETTER TO WHITE WOMAN

May 9, unknown Negro, West Texas.

GIVING INFORMATION

July 12, James Nelson, Abbeyville, S.C.

STEALING

Jan. 5, Alfred Davis, Live Oak County, Ark.

LARCENY

April 18, Henry Montgomery, Lewisburg, Tenn.

POLITICAL CAUSES

July 19, John Brownlee, Oxford, Ala.

CONJURING

July 20, Allen Myers, Rankin County, Miss.

ATTEMPTED MURDER

June 1, Frank Ballard, Jackson, Tenn.

ALLEGED MURDER

April 5, Negro, near Selma, Ala.; April 5, Negro, near Selma, Ala.

WITHOUT CAUSE

May 17, Samuel Wood, Gates City, Va.

BARN BURNING

April 22, Thomas Black, Tuscumbia, Ala.; April 22, John Williams, Tuscumbia, Ala.; April 22, Toney Johnson, Tuscumbia, Ala.; July 14, William Bell, Dixon, Tenn.; Sept. 1, Daniel Hawkins, Millington, Tenn.; Sept. 1, Robert Haynes, Millington, Tenn.; Sept. 1, Warner Williams, Millington, Tenn.; Sept. 1, Edward Hall, Millington, Tenn.; Sept. 1, John Haynes, Millington, Tenn.; Sept. 1, Graham White, Millington, Tenn.

ASKING WHITE WOMAN TO MARRY HIM

May 23, William Brooks, Galesline, Ark.

OFFENSES CHARGED FOR LYNCHING

Suspected arson, 2; stealing, 1; political causes, 1; murder, 45; rape, 29; desperado, 1; suspected incendiarism, 1; train wrecking, 1; enticing servant away, 1; kidnapping, 1; unknown offense, 6; larceny, 1; barn burning, 10; writing letters to a white woman, 1; without cause, 1; burglary, 1; asking white woman to marry, 1; conspiracy, 1; attempted murder, 1; horse stealing, 3; highway robbery, 1; alleged rape, 1; attempted rape, 11; race prejudice, 2; introducing smallpox, 1; giving information, 1; conjuring, 1; incendiarism, 2; arson, 1; assault, 1; no offense, 1; alleged murder, 2; total (colored), 134.

LYNCHING STATES

Mississippi, 15; Arkansas, 8; Virginia, 5; Tennessee, 15; Alabama, 12; Kentucky, 12; Texas, 9; Georgia, 19; South Carolina, 5; Florida, 7; Louisiana, 15; Missouri, 4; Ohio, 2; Maryland, 1; West Virginia, 2; Indiana, 1; Kansas, 1; Pennsylvania, 1.

LYNCHING BY THE MONTH

January, 11; February, 17; March, 8; April, 36; May, 16; June, 31; July, 21; August, 4; September, 17; October, 7; November, 9; December, 20; total colored and white, 197.

WOMEN LYNCHED

July 24, unknown woman, race prejudice, Sampson County, Miss.; March 6, unknown, woman, unknown offense, Marche, Ark.; Dec. 5, Mrs. Teddy Arthur, unknown cause, Lincoln County, W. Va.

10

THE REMEDY

It is a well-established principle of law that every wrong has a remedy. Herein rests our respect for law. The Negro does not claim that all of the one thousand black men, women and children, who have been hanged, shot and burned alive during the past ten years, were innocent of the charges made against them. We have associated too long with the white man not to have copied his vices as well as his virtues. But we do insist that the punishment is not the same for both classes of criminals. In lynching, opportunity is not given the Negro to defend himself against the unsupported accusations of white men and women. The word of the accuser is held to be true and the excited bloodthirsty mob demands that the rule of law be reversed and instead of proving the accused to be guilty, the victim of their hate and revenge must prove himself innocent. No evidence he can offer will satisfy the mob; he is bound hand and foot and swung into eternity. Then to excuse its infamy, the mob almost invariably reports the monstrous falsehood that its victim made a full confession before he was hanged.

With all military, legal and political power in their hands, only two of the lynching States have attempted a check by exercising the power which is theirs. Mayor Trout, of Roanoke, Virginia, called out the militia in 1893, to protect a Negro prisoner, and in so doing nine men were killed and a number wounded. Then the mayor and militia withdrew, left the Negro to his fate and he was promptly lynched. The business men realized the blow to the town's were given light sentences, the highest being one of twelve financial interests, called the mayor home, the grand jury indicted and prosecuted the ringleaders of the mob. They months in State prison. The day he arrived at the penitentiary, he was pardoned by the governor of the State.

The only other real attempt made by the authorities to protect a prisoner of the law, and which was more successful, was that of Gov. McKinley, of Ohio, who sent the militia to Washington Courthouse, O., in October, 1894, and five men were killed and twenty wounded in maintaining the principle that the law must be upheld.

In South Carolina, in April, 1893, Gov. Tillman aided the mob by yielding up to be killed, a prisoner of the law, who had voluntarily placed himself under the Governor's protection. Public sentiment by its representatives has encouraged Lynch Law, and upon the revolution of this sentiment we must depend for its abolition.

Therefore, we demand a fair trial by law for those accused of crime, and punishment by law after honest conviction. No maudlin sympathy for criminals is solicited, but we do ask that the law shall punish all alike. We earnestly desire those that control the forces which make public sentiment to join with us in the demand. Surely the humanitarian spirit of this country which reaches out to denounce the treatment of the Russian Jews, the Armenian Christians, the laboring poor of Europe, the Siberian exiles and the native women of India—will not longer refuse to lift its voice on this subject. If it were known that the cannibals or the savage Indians had burned three human beings alive in the past two years, the whole of Christendom would be roused, to devise ways and means to put a stop to it. Can you remain silent and inactive when such things are done in our own community and country? Is your duty to humanity in the United States less binding?

What can you do, reader, to prevent lynching, to thwart anarchy and promote law and order throughout our land?

1st. You can help disseminate the facts contained in this book by bringing them to the knowledge of every one with whom you come in contact, to the end that public sentiment may be revolutionized. Let the facts speak for themselves, with you as a medium.

2d. You can be instrumental in having churches, missionary societies, Y.M.C.A.'s, W.C.T.U.'s and all Christian and moral forces in connection with your religious and social life, pass resolutions of condemnation and protest every time a lynching takes place; and see that they axe sent to the place where these outrages occur.

3d. Bring to the intelligent consideration of Southern people the refusal of capital to invest where lawlessness and mob violence hold sway. Many labor organizations have declared by resolution that they would avoid lynch infested localities as they would the pestilence when seeking new homes. If the South wishes to build up its waste places quickly, there is no better way than to uphold the majesty of the law by enforcing obedience to the same, and meting out the same punishment to all classes of criminals, white as well as black. "Equality before the law," must become a fact as well as a theory before America is truly the "land of the free and the home of the brave."

4th. Think and act on independent lines in this behalf, remembering that after all, it is the white man's civilization and the white man's government which are on trial. This crusade will determine whether that civilization can maintain itself by itself, or whether anarchy shall prevail; Whether this Nation shall write itself down a success at self government, or in deepest humiliation admit its failure complete; whether the precepts and theories of Christianity are professed and practiced by American white people as Golden Rules of thought and action, or adopted as a system of morals to be preached to, heathen until they attain to the intelligence which needs the system of Lynch Law.

5th. Congressman Blair offered a resolution in the House of Representatives, August, 1894. The organized life of the country can speedily make this a law by sending resolutions to Congress indorsing Mr. Blair's bill and asking Congress to create the commission. In no better way can the question be settled, and the Negro does not fear the issue. The following is the resolution:

Resolved, By the House of Representatives and Senate in congress assembled, That the committee on labor be instructed to investigate and report the number, location and date of all alleged assaults by males upon females throughout the country during the ten years last preceding the passing of this joint resolution, for or on account of which organized but unlawful violence has been inflicted or attempted to be inflicted. Also to ascertain and report all facts of organized but unlawful violence to the person, with the attendant facts and circumstances, which have been inflicted upon accused persons alleged to have been guilty of crimes punishable by due process of law which have taken place in any part of the country within the ten years last preceding the passage of this resolution. Such investigation shall be made by the usual methods and agencies of the Department of Labor, and report made to Congress as soon as the work can be satisfactorily done, and the sum of $25,000, or so much thereof as may be necessary, is hereby appropriated to pay the expenses out of any money in the treasury not otherwise appropriated.

The belief has been constantly expressed in England that in the United States, which has produced Wm. Lloyd Garrison, Henry Ward Beecher, James Russell Lowell, John G. Whittier and Abraham Lincoln there must be those of their descendants who would take hold of the work of inaugurating an era of law and order. The colored people of this country who have been loyal to the flag believe the same, and strong in that belief have begun this crusade. To those who still feel they have no obligation in the matter, we commend the following lines of Lowell on "Freedom."

Men! whose boast it is that ye
Come of fathers brave and free,
If there breathe on earth a slave
Are ye truly free and brave?
If ye do not feel the chain,
When it works a brother's pain,
Are ye not base slaves indeed,
Slaves unworthy to be freed?

Women! who shall one day bear
Sons to breathe New England air,
If ye hear without a blush,
Deeds to make the roused blood rush
Like red lava through your veins,
For your sisters now in chains,—
Answer! are ye fit to be
Mothers of the brave and free?

Is true freedom but to break
Fetters for our own dear sake,
And, with leathern hearts, forget

That we owe mankind a debt?
No! true freedom is to share
All the chains our brothers wear,
And, with heart and hand, to be
Earnest to make others free!

There are slaves who fear to speak
For the fallen and the weak;
They are slaves who will not choose
Hatred, scoffing, and abuse,
Rather than in silence shrink
From the truth they needs must think;
They are slaves who dare not be
In the right with two or three.

A FIELD FOR PRACTICAL WORK

The very frequent inquiry made after my lectures by interested friends is "What can I do to help the cause?" The answer always is: "Tell the world the facts." When the Christian world knows the alarming growth and extent of outlawry in our land, some means will be found to stop it.

The object of this publication is to tell the facts, and friends of the cause can lend a helping hand by aiding in the distribution of these books. When I present our cause to a minister, editor, lecturer, or representative of any moral agency, the first demand is for facts and figures. Plainly, I can not then hand out a book with a twenty-five-cent tariff on the information contained. This would be only a new method in the book agents' art. In all such cases it is a pleasure to submit this book for investigation, with the certain assurance of gaining a friend to the cause.

There are many agencies which may be enlisted in our cause by the general circulation of the facts herein contained. The preachers, teachers, editors and humanitarians of the white race, at home and abroad, must have facts laid before them, and it is our duty to supply these facts. The Central Anti-Lynching League, Room 9, 128 Clark St., Chicago, has established a Free Distribution Fund, the work of which can be promoted by all who are interested in this work.

Antilynching leagues, societies and individuals can order books from this fund at agents' rates. The books will be sent to their order, or, if desired, will be distributed by the League among those whose cooperative aid we so greatly need. The writer hereof assures prompt distribution of books according to order, and public acknowledgment of all orders through the public press.

Printed in the United States
131327LV00004B/163/A

9 781846 375927